The Gentleman's Journey to Success

ESSENTIAL MANNERS AND SOCIAL
SKILLS YOU NEED TO SUCCEED

Patricia Napier-Fitzpatrick

Copyright© 2021 Patricia Napier-Fitzpatrick

All rights reserved. No part of this book may be reproducedin any manner whatsoever without permission except in case of brief quotations embodied in critical articles of review.

The Etiquette School of New York in Manhattan and Southampton
243 Elm Street, Southampton, NY 11968

Editor: Nanci Alderman

Visit my website at www.etiquette-ny.com

ISBN: 978-0-578-94184-4 (paperback)

FIRST EDITION: August 2021

*For My Husband, Jay
My Brothers, Ed and Bill
My Nephews, Tommy, Paul, Ross, and Billy*

*And for every man who is on his personal
journey to success*

Contents

Acknowledgments	ix
Preface	xi
Introduction	xiii
Etiquette: Past and Present Civility and Decorum	xv
The Stages of a Man's Life	xix
The Road Not Taken	xxi

Part One: The Making of the Man: Your Guide to Personal Development

1	The A–Z Personal Qualities Successful Men Possess with Inspirational Quotes	3
2	You'll Never Get a Second Chance to Make a First Impression	15
3	Make an Excellent Impression with Your Polished, Powerful Presence	17
4	Upgrade Your Style and Grooming to Be Seen and Heard as a Winner	21
5	Be Fashion Conscious and Observe Dress Codes	25
6	The Importance of Confident Body Language	31
7	Enhance All Your Relationships with Refined Social Graces	37
8	Create a Positive, First-Class Vocal Image	41
9	Take Charge of your Attitude	45
10	Step into Life with Confidence	47
11	Build Rapport to Connect with Others	51
12	Be Charming to Be More Likeable	55
13	Recognize and Manage Emotions with Your EQ Skills	59
14	Be an Inspirational Leader and Team Builder	63

15	Form Productive Habits and Effective Time Management Skills	69
16	Define Your Personal Brand to Discover What Makes You Unique	75
17	Become an Effective Communicator	79

Part Two: Your Guide to the Business World

18	Thrive in the Business World with Honed Soft Skills	87
19	Master the Art of Courteous Greetings and Smooth Introductions	93
20	Make Artful Small Talk and Polite Conversation	101
21	Mingle with Ease and Grace at Networking and Social Business Functions	107
22	Formal Onsite Business Meeting Protocol	113
23	Virtual Business Meeting Protocol	117
24	Be the Quintessential Professional at the Office	123
25	Polished, Professional Business Communications	129
26	Social Media and Networking Guidelines to Follow	135
27	Outshine the Competition to Land a Job	139
28	What New College Graduates Need to Know and Do to Launch Successful Careers	147

Part Three: Your Etiquette Guide to the Social World

29	Be a Courteous Man About Town	153
30	A Modern Manners Checklist for Young Men	157
31	Be a Gentleman with a Lady	163
32	Show Consideration to Your Fellow Gym-Goers	169
33	A Gentleman's Sport: Courteous Decorum for the Golf Course	173
34	Dignified Decorum for Attending the Opera, Ballet, Symphony or Theater	177
35	Civil Conduct for Private and Commercial Air Travel	181
36	A Savvy Man's Guide to Hosting or Attending a Party	183

37	Houseguest Guidelines for Enjoyable Visits with Family and Friends	189
38	Make a Favorable Impression at the Table	193
39	How to Host a Flawless Meal at a Restaurant	197
40	Show Your Appreciation with a Thoughtful Thank-You Note	203
41	Pursue Culture to Enrich Yourself and Become a More Interesting, Knowledgeable Man	205

Acknowledgments

First and foremost, I wish to thank my editor and good friend, Nanci Alderman, for her invaluable help and delightful camaraderie while working on this book. It was improved immeasurably by her insights, research, and excellent and meticulous editing.

I am especially indebted to my husband, Jay, for his unfailing patience, support, and design input. And, I would also like to express my appreciation to my siblings who have always encouraged me in my endeavors, and have happily provided feedback when asked. They, along with my husband and daughter, Kelly, have always been my greatest advocates and I will forever be grateful to them.

And a special note of thanks to the men and women who have attended my workshops and seminars through the years, where I was able to test my ideas and learn from their questions and insights. It has truly been a joy to meet and get to know them.

Preface

When one thinks of manners, one often thinks of the South—Southern manners, Southern charm—where warm smiles, courteous behavior, and all-around niceties abound. But I have found the possession of good manners to be ubiquitous across states, across countries, and where you least expect to find them. Of course, there is always the exception of someone being rude or unkind anywhere one goes; but if we model the civil and kind behavior that we would like others to follow, we can help make the world a better place.

As the eldest of six siblings, I learned from an early age that if I wanted my brothers and sisters to behave nicely, I would need to behave nicely as well—to set an example for them to follow. And today, I am just as passionate about sharing my ideals as I was then and striving to set a worthy example for all to follow.

For the past nearly fifteen years, I have had the privilege of meeting with countless young people and adults for social etiquette and business protocol instruction. I have presented etiquette and protocol seminars and workshops to corporations, academia, private clubs and countless individuals in the New York City area, as well as a great many individuals from other states and countries. I have also been invited to share my expertise with such noteworthy publications as the *New York Times, Financial Times, Business Week*, the *Wall Street Journal*, and many other respected publications. And I have appeared on nearly all major network and cable news shows.

Prior to founding The Etiquette School of New York, I worked as a marketing executive in New York City where I learned—mostly by trial and error and observation—how to navigate the corporate world. I often tell my twenty-somethings and university students that I wish I had known then what I know now—what I am teaching them.

Much of what you will read in this book has been taught to those with whom I have met for etiquette instruction. Knowing that not everyone is afforded the opportunity to attend courses such as those The Etiquette School of New York offers, I wrote *The Gentleman's Journey to Success—Essential Manners and Social Skills You Need to Succeed* to share this valuable and empowering knowledge. And although I have directed this book to men, it doesn't mean women would not gain equally from its empowering guidelines—just as over 90 percent of the book I wrote for women several years ago, *"Proper, Poised, and Polished—The Power of You,"* is equally valuable for men. It is primarily the style sections in these books that make them gender specific.

This book does not strive to provide all the etiquette rules or manners for every possible topic or situation you may encounter in your life. I have selectively chosen the subjects I believe are most relevant for the twenty-first century man. For a comprehensive guide to nearly every possible situation where etiquette rules and manners need to be employed, I recommend acquiring *Emily Post's Etiquette 19th Edition: Manners for Today*.

Furthermore, this book is much more than an etiquette book. It is modeled after my "Social Success Makeover—Finishing School for Adults" course which, in addition to providing essential etiquette and protocol knowledge, equips students with the refined social graces, polished presence, and leaderships skills that enable them to feel confident and at ease in their personal and professional lives, and to be successful in becoming their unique, personal best.

One last note: This book is not necessarily meant to be read from beginning to end. Read the chapters that appeal to you or that you feel would be of the most help at a particular point on your journey. Think of it as a reference book to be kept and referred to periodically.

The joy is in the journey. Enjoy yours! I wish you much success along the way!

Patricia Napier-Fitzpatrick

Introduction

The Gentleman's Journey to Success: Essential Manners and Social Skills You Need to Succeed was written to inspire and motivate men to take charge of their unique journey through life, and to excite and challenge them with the idea that they are in complete control of how successful they will be in achieving their personal best. In other words, your destination is yours to shape. What an empowering thought!

This book will provide you with the tools, knowledge, and leadership skills you need on this journey. Confidence, polished social skills, and the awareness and application of the simple rules of courtesy will greatly assist and guide you toward achieving your dreams. Wherever you happen to be on your journey now, there are steps you can take to transform your life. Carpe diem.

Success in any form is a process. In order to have a successful journey, you have to be fully prepared for all eventualities. Consider the steps you will take along the way: some small, some big, some unplanned. You have to look at the bigger picture and visualize the end in your mind so you stay committed to achieving your desired destination.

The temptation to take the easy road is always there. It is as easy as staying in bed in the morning and sleeping. But discipline is paramount to ultimate success and victory for any leader and any team.

—Jocko Willink

Having a clear and defined road map or strategy is essential. Do you have a mission statement that clearly defines who you are as a person, identifies your purpose in life, and how you aim to pursue that purpose?

It's important because it will help you focus on how to meet both your short- and long-term goals, and will serve as a guidepost for where you want to go in life.

On any journey, a traveler needs to review his map often to make sure he is still on course. If he has lost his sense of direction and veered off course, he will need to make alternative plans—ones that will nevertheless result in a positive, if perhaps somewhat different, outcome than originally planned. Think about what might go wrong along the way so you can mitigate any challenges

> *Every journey that is successful has culs-de-sac and speed bumps.*
> —Peter Guber

Whatever your ultimate destination, chances are someone has been there before you. Let them guide you. It should ease your mind to know that many who have come before you have had unexpected delays or obstacles placed in their way before reaching their goal; and that it isn't always a direct route to achieving success. Life is about the choices you make. If you make the right choices, you will have a productive, fulfilling, happy life. You want to enjoy it, regardless of how hard it is.

> *No one can make you successful; the will to success comes from within.*
> —Fabrizio Moreira

Etiquette: Past and Present Civility and Decorum

Etiquette is the science of living. It embraces everything. It is ethics. It is honor.

—Emily Post

A Brief History of Etiquette

The original etiquette manuals of Western civilization were medieval success manuals for knights. There was not an authentic knight's code of chivalry as such, however; it was more of a moral system that went beyond rules of combat and introduced the concept of chivalrous conduct. The chivalric code was developed between 1170 and 1220. Its focus was on the ideals of chivalry idealized by knighthood such as bravery, courtesy, honor, and gallantry toward women.

The first actual record of American etiquette was George Washington's *Rules of Civility* written around 1744. His book is a list of 110 rules of polite behavior one should follow: They are based on a set of rules composed by the French Jesuits in the late 16th century, and were presumed to have been copied out as part of an exercise in penmanship. The list included guidelines for behavior in pleasant company, appropriate actions in formal situations, and general courtesies. One such courtesy was:

Every action done in company ought to be with some sign of respect to those that are present.

—George Washington

Today there are many books on etiquette. Over the years, the subject matter has been greatly expanded to encompass all areas of our personal and professional lives. Modern etiquette books and the rules they contain derive from traditional rules of polite behavior and apply them to contemporary life. These are not rules dreamed up to make our lives more difficult; they are devised to make our lives better and go more smoothly. They provide structure and prevent chaos, and make life more pleasant for all.

Why is it important to know and follow the societal rules for civility and acceptable decorum? Etiquette is a code that governs social behavior. It is a set of rules, or guidelines, to help steer our interactions with others. Manners are how we apply those rules. Good manners are based on kindness, consideration and respect for others. A person can only go so far without good manners, and there is no economic barrier to having them. As Clarence Thomas once said, "Good manners can open doors that the best education cannot." Learning how to show respect, consideration and compassion, as well as knowing how to work graciously with people who are different from you, are incredibly important qualities to possess.

Good manners and civil behavior are not only indispensable in your personal life, they play an invaluable role in your professional life as well, since what it takes to succeed in social settings is equally important in the business world. Impeccable manners and the ability to move with ease and grace in all social arenas are essential attributes of successful people. If you are articulate and well dressed, and back that up with social graces, admirable personality traits, and the knowledge needed to succeed in your chosen field, you will be welcome wherever you choose to go.

Nearly all executives agree that handling oneself well at a cocktail party or dinner is at least as important as handling oneself skillfully in the boardroom. After all, more business connections are made and deals closed at the dinner table or on the golf course than in the office. Possessing etiquette and social skills can increase confidence in all aspects of your life. Etiquette enhances any social situation by encouraging inclusiveness and positive personal connections with others.

Regardless of the industry in which you work, people prefer to do business with people they like and with whom they feel comfortable. Treating others with respect and courtesy; knowing how to comport yourself in a socially-skillful, appropriate way; and knowing how to build rapport in a wide variety of social and business settings will enable you to build solid, productive relationships that lead to professional success. Showing the same consideration and respect for your family, friends, and significant others will also lead to a fulfilling and happy personal life.

So how does technology play into this? Technology is continually changing the way we interact—both socially and professionally—and it can be challenging to know how to conduct oneself in a way society deems appropriate in a given situation. Although the spirit of etiquette always remains essentially the same, the expression of etiquette—the rules of conduct which govern social life and our associations with one another—is forever evolving to adjust to the times. These times are no different in that etiquette experts are continuously updating the modern rules for acceptable interactions with others–whether you are online or off. It is also important to keep in mind that etiquette rules and manners may, and often do, differ by culture, and it is wise to learn what other cultures consider appropriate social behavior in order to foster good social and professional relationships.

Although some think manners are less important in today's fast-paced, technology-centered world, they could not be more mistaken. Good manners will always be considered a desirable trait in a person, and all the more appreciated in today's often less-than-civil, harried society.

> *Your manners are always under examination, and by committees little suspected, awarding or denying very high prizes when you least think it.*
> —Ralph Waldo Emerson

The Stages of a Man's Life

In his play *As You Like It*, William Shakespeare writes of seven distinct stages, or acts, through which a man progresses. His viewpoint of the cycle of life is presented in Jacques' soliloquy "The Seven Ages of Man," which begins with the famous line "All the world's a stage." There is a sculpture in London by Richard Kindersley that depicts these seven ages.

A more contemporary view is described by Daniel L Levinson in *The Seasons of a Man's Life*, his highly praised and thoroughly researched book on the patterns of adult development. In it he writes of four major seasons in a man's life. The first is childhood and adolescence, from ages 0-22; the second is early adulthood, ages 22-45; the third spans middle adulthood, ages 40 to 65; and the fourth season is late adulthood, ages 65 and up.

Mr. Levinson writes: "There is this idea of seasons: a series of periods or stages within the life cycle. The process is not a continuous, unchanging flow. The eras are partially overlapping, so that a new one is getting underway as the previous one is terminating. The transition between eras consistently takes four or five years—not less than three and rarely more than six. Each phase in the life cycle has its own virtues and limitations."

What I believe is that, as you mature and develop skills to navigate the world of adulthood, if you maintain the wonder, curiosity, enthusiasm, and pleasures of discovery you had as a child, you will always be relevant and valued.

The Road Not Taken

—Robert Frost

Two roads diverged in a yellow wood
And sorry I could not travel both
And be one traveler, long I stood
And looked down one as far as I could
To where it bent in the undergrowth;

Then took the other, as just as fair,
And having perhaps the better claim,
Because it was grassy and wanted wear;
Though as for that the passing there
Had worn them really about the same,

And both that morning equally lay
In leaves no step had trodden black.
Oh, I kept the first for another day!
Yet knowing how way leads on to way,
I doubted if I should ever come back.

I shall be telling this with a sigh
Somewhere ages and ages hence:
Two roads diverged in a wood, and I—
I took the one less traveled by,
And that has made all the difference.

PART ONE

The Making of the Man: Your Guide to Personal Development

1
SUCCESS

The A–Z Personal Qualities Successful Men Possess with Inspirational Quotes

A
APPRECIATIVE

Gratitude is the healthiest of all human emotions. The more you express gratitude for what you have, the more likely you will have even more to express gratitude for.
Zig Ziglar

Being polite and grateful will make other people willing to help. And if people are willing to help you, you may accidentally get something you want.
Jason Sudeikis

The way to develop the best that is in a person is by appreciation and encouragement.
Charles Schwab

B
BELIEVABLE

To be persuasive, we must be believable; to be believable, we must be credible; to be credible, we must be truthful.
Edward R. Murrow

Whatever you do, you have to be believable for this is the prerequisite of credibility and relevance.
Richard Mwebesa

Few things detract more from your credibility and the respect of your colleagues and peers than being called on the carpet to deflect accusations and defend an untruth.
Mark Goulston

C
CHARMING

Let's be grateful to people who make us happy, they are the charming gardeners who make our souls blossom.
Marcel Proust

It's absurd to divide people into good or bad. People are either charming or tedious.
Oscar Wilde

Charm is the ability to make someone think that both of you are special.
Amiel Henri Frederic

D
DISCIPLINED

We are what we repeatedly do. Excellence then, is not an act, but a habit.
Aristotle

The richest inheritance any child can have is a stable, loving, disciplined family life.
Daniel Patrick Moynihan

Only the disciplined ones in life are free. If you are undisciplined, you are a slave to your moods and passions.
Eliud Kipchoge

E
EMOTIONALLY INTELLIGENT

If your emotional abilities aren't in hand, if you don't have self-awareness, if you are not able to manage your distressing emotions, if you can't have empathy and have effective relationships, no matter how smart you are, you are not going to get very far.
Daniel Goleman

When dealing with people, remember you are not dealing with creatures of logic, but with creatures of emotion.
Dale Carnegie

No one cares how much you know, until they know how much you care.
Theodore Roosevelt

F
FASHION CONSCIOUS

Fashion is the armor to survive everyday life.
Bill Cunningham

Don't be into trends. Don't make fashion own you, but you decide who you are, what you want to express by the way you dress, and the way you live.
Gianni Versace

Good grooming is integral and impeccable stye is a must. If you don't look the part, no one will want to give you time or money.
Daymond John

G
GENTLEMAN

The final test of a gentleman is his respect for those who can be of no use to him.
William Lyon Phillips

Character. Intelligence. Strength. Style. That makes a gentleman.
Louis Raphael

I was brought up to be a gentleman. That means you know how to walk, talk, and dress the part.
Brian McKnight

H
HONORABLE

Keep your word. Honor commitments and they will double back to honor you.
Bill Rancic

Of all the properties which belong to honorable men, no one is so highly prized as character.
Henry Clay

The real benefit of being honorable isn't how others view you, but rather, in how you view yourself.
Dennis Prager

I
INTERESTING

Develop interest in life as you see it, in people, things, literature, music—the world is so rich, simply throbbing with rich treasures, beautiful souls and interesting people. Forget yourself.
Henry Miller

Interesting people have a special magnetism. They tell incredible stories and lead unusual lives. They're curious more than anything else.
Travis Bradberry

*B*eing a global citizen makes you a more interesting person.
Joe Russ

J
JUDICIOUS

*T*o be known as a man of sound judgement will be much in your favor.
Grantland Rice

*M*aybe the greatest power of all is the power of restraint.
Craig D. Lounsbrough

*C*riticism is, or ought to be, a judicious act.
Amitava Kumer

K
KNOWLEDGEABLE

*K*nowledge is power. Information is liberating. Education is the promise of progress in every society, in every family.
Kofi Annan

*I*n my whole life, I have known no wise people (over a broad subject matter area) who didn't read all the time—none, zero.
Charlie Munger

*M*y biggest motivation? Just to keep challenging myself. I see life almost like one long university education that I never had—every day I'm learning something new.
Richard Branson

L
LEADER

*O*utstanding leaders go out of their way to boost the self-esteem of their personnel. If people believe in themselves, it's amazing what they can accomplish.
Sam Walton

*T*he supreme quality for leadership is unquestionably integrity. Without it, no real success is possible, no matter whether it is on a section gang, a football field, in an army, or in an office.
Dwight D. Eisenhower

*T*he challenge of leadership is to be strong, but not rude; be kind, but not weak; be bold, but not a bully; be thoughtful, but not lazy; be humble, but not timid; be proud, but not arrogant; have humor, but without folly.
Jim Rohn

M
MANNERLY

I seek constantly to improve my manners and graces, for they are the sugar to which all are attracted.
Og Mandino

*G*ood manners are appreciated as much as bad manners are abhorred.
Bryant H. McGill

*I*t is so important to have manners and treat people from all walks of life the way they should be treated.
David Beckham

N
NOBLE

Believe in something big. Your life is worth a noble motive.
Walter I. Anderson

There is nothing noble in being superior to your fellow man. True nobility lies in being superior to yourself.
Ernest Hemingway

A noble purpose inspires a sacrifice, stimulates innovation, and encourages perseverance.
Gary Hamel

O
OPEN-MINDED

Education's purpose is to replace an empty mind with an open mind.
Malcolm Forbes

The future belongs to those who see possibilities before they become obvious.
John Scully

I'm open for possibilities, for choices. I always welcome new ideas. I'm always eager to learn. I'm never going to close my mind from learning.
Cesar Millan

P
POLISHED

Good grooming and hygiene are essential. It's never too early to start being concerned about your appearance—first impressions are everything.
Robert Parish

*T*he polished professional begins with the perfect ensemble. The days of the strict suit and tie dress code may be waning, but that doesn't mean there shouldn't be room for a tailored suit in your wardrobe.
Nunzio Bagnato

*M*ake sure your appearance is appropriate for the setting and the company culture, and that it is consistent with others at the level you aspire to. Pay attention to your clothing choices, tailoring and grooming, and make sure there's nothing about your appearance that will distract from the impression you want to leave.
Grant Power

Q
QUALITY

*Q*uality means doing it right when no one is looking.
Henry Ford

*Q*uality is never an accident. It is always the result of intelligent effort.
John Ruskin

*B*e a yardstick of quality. Some people aren't used to an environment where excellence is expected.
Steve Jobs

R
RESPECTFUL

*R*espect for ourselves guides our morals, respect for others guides our manners.
Laurence Sterne

*S*elf-respect is earned by being better than you used to be, by being dependable in times of testing, straight in times of temptation.
David Brooks

Everyone in society should be a role model, not only for their self-respect, but for respect from others.
Barry Bonds

S
SELF-CONFIDENT

One important key to success is self-confidence. An important key to self-confidence is preparedness.
Arthur Ashe

Believe in yourself! Have faith in your abilities. Without a humble but reasonable confidence in your own powers you cannot be successful or happy.
Norman Vincent Peale

Positivity, confidence, and persistence are key in life, so never give up on yourself.
Khalid

T
TEAM PLAYER

Great things in business are never done by one person. They're done by a team of people.
Steve Jobs

Talent wins games, but teamwork and intelligence wins championships.
Michael Jordan

A team is not a group of people who work together. A team is a group of people who trust each other.
Simon Sinek

U
UNDERSTANDING

A successful life is one that is lived through understanding and pursuing one's own path, not chasing after the dreams of others.
Chin-Ning Chu

To effectively communicate, we must realize that we are all different in the way we perceive the world and use this understanding as a guide to our communication with others.
Tony Robbins

Successful negotiation is not about getting to 'yes'; it's about mastering 'no' and understanding what the path to an agreement is.
Christopher Voss

V
VISIONARY

A visionary is someone who can see the future, or thinks he sees the future. In my case, I use it and it comes out right. That doesn't come from daydreams or dreams, but it comes from knowing the market and knowing the world and knowing people really well and knowing where they're going to be tomorrow.
Leonard Lauder

Visionary people face the same problems everyone else faces; but rather than get paralyzed by their problems, visionaries immediately commit themselves to finding a solution.
Bill Hybel

Someone's sitting in the shade today because someone planted a tree a long time ago.
Warren Buffet

W
WELL-SPOKEN

In the pursuit of becoming a better man, becoming well-spoken is a task that should not be overlooked.
Brett McKay

Everyone needs to learn how to communicate their ideas clearly and professionally. One who speaks clearly and confidently automatically commands respect. That's a quality that all great leaders possess."
Lenny Laskowski

Good English, well-spoken and well written, will open more doors than a college degree. Bad English will slam doors you didn't even know existed.
William Raspberry

X
X-FACTOR

People do not decide to become extraordinary. They decide to accomplish extraordinary things.
Edmund Hillary

Desire, burning desire, is basic to achieving anything beyond the ordinary.
Joseph B. Wirthlin

Do not be afraid of greatness; some are born to greatness, some achieve greatness, and others have greatness thrust upon them.
Shakespeare

Y
YOUTHFUL

It is never wise to discourage youthful idealism.
Stephen Kinzer

Hold onto your dream. Don't let past failures or dire economic forecasts make you a pessimist. Keep your youthful dreams alive and create your own opportunities.
Paul Zane Pilzer

I'm still growing. I take each day, one day-at-a-time. I'm always thinking and dreaming. As long as this heart keeps beating, there will be new things coming along.
Roy Haynes

Z
ZESTFUL

True happiness comes from the joy of deeds well done, the zest of creating things new.
Antoine de Saint-Exupery

If you have zest and enthusiasm, you attract zest and enthusiasm. Life does give back in kind.
Norman Vincent Peale

Good humor is a tonic for the mind and body. It is the best antidote for anxiety and depression. It is a business asset. It attracts and keeps friends. It lightens human burdens. It is the direct route to serenity and contentment.
Grenville Kleiser

2

|SUCCESS|

You'll Never Get a Second Chance to Make a First Impression

> *A first impression is the most important impression you'll ever make—and you only get one chance to make it. Business deals can be made or broken, first dates become second dates or not, friendships are created or fail to form; everything hinges on that all-important initial encounter.*
> —Ann Demarais, Ph.D., and Valerie White, Ph.D.,
> *First Impressions*

YOU HAVE THREE SECONDS TO get it right! Positive or negative impressions are made by the first contact between two people. The first contact may be written, by telephone, in-person, or virtually.

- **According to researchers at Harvard University, we decide if we believe someone, like someone, and trust someone before we have even heard them speak.**
  And, we make those judgments in the first few seconds of meeting and rarely change them.

- **Appearance counts for 55% of the impression you make. The attitude you project, both verbally and nonverbally, counts for 38%; and lastly, what you say only accounts for 7%.**
  Yes, 93% of a first impression is nonverbal.

- **Image is the impression you make on others and it is in your control.**
  It is the tangible quality you project that people respond to emotionally and intellectually.

- **If you have a very positive trait—if you are smart, handsome, funny, kind, and so forth—you are likely to be perceived as having other positive traits.**
  It is called the "halo effect."

- **Social media can count as a first impression, since most people will Google you before meeting you.**
  Be sure the impression you convey on social media will ensure you are given a chance to meet in person.

- **Meetings and conferences are often held virtually now.**
  Follow the same guidelines for these meetings that you would for an in-person meeting. Grooming, attire, body language, and what you say will make a positive or negative impression.

3
SUCCESS

Make an Excellent Impression with Your Polished, Powerful Presence

Polished: Accomplished and skillful.

Powerful: Having control and influence over people and events.

Presence: A noteworthy quality of poise and effectiveness.

Presenting You:

WE LIVE IN A FAST-PACED, global society and people make instant judgments about you that can either open doors for you or close them. Priceless opportunities have been lost for individuals because they have not paid attention to their most visible asset—their presence. Very few degrees or skills can compensate for a poor impression, inadequate social skills, or weak non-verbal communication. And on a personal level, your presence is just as important. It can either work for you or keep people from wanting to get to know you.

Clothing is transformative. It affects how you feel about yourself and your relationship to the world. It doesn't matter where you've come from. It only matters where you are going. You can become the person you want to be by dressing the part, walking the walk, and backing up your polished presence with a respectful and kind regard for others.

A polished, powerful presence rests on three pillars:

1. **Appearance**

    - **How you look is important, not only in first impressions, but also in ongoing interactions.**
    It is the filter through which your talent and suitability will be evaluated, and remains one of the main factors that will encourage others to want to work with you or for you. Package yourself to succeed in your chosen field on a consistent basis.

    - **Look appropriate for your environment and the occasion.**
    Showing an appreciation for time and place is reflected in your appearance. When you follow the established dress codes for your workplace and dress as requested for events, it demonstrates your good will and acknowledgment of the importance of fitting it with society's expectations.

    - **Be well groomed and fit.**
    Being well groomed is just as important—if not more so—than being appropriately dressed. Styled hair, well-tended nails, good breath, clean, pressed clothes, and polished shoes are a must. In fact, in a recent survey of senior leaders in the U.S., more than a third considered polish and grooming vital to a man or woman making a good impression. And today, more emphasis is being placed on being and looking fit for a job. The workplace is more stressful today than ever. Exercising and eating right will help you meet the demands of your job, as well as add significantly to the impression you make on others.

2. **Attitude / Body Language**

   - **Your attitude signals to others how you feel about yourself, the situation, and them.**
   The entrance you make, your posture, your eye contact, the way you shake hands, the way you introduce yourself and others, how you perform your job functions and interact with your colleagues all convey a message about your attitude.

   - **Your body language either confirms or contradicts your powerful image.**
   Nonverbal cues such as the way you stand, your head movements, facial expressions, and gestures subconsciously confirm or contradict in the mind of the observer the visual message you convey by the way you are dressed.

3. **Actions**

   - **Every verbal encounter, whether face-to-face or in the virtual world, is an all-important opportunity to create and nurture a positive impression.**
   Your communication skills, both verbal and nonverbal, are what ultimately win you the attention and favorable opinion of colleagues, clients, and friends.

   - **Being courteous and treating people with respect will be noticed and work in your favor, just as poor manners will work against you.**
   Good manners and consideration for others are timeless; and those who recognize that will find themselves not only sought after and promoted, but more importantly, at ease in any social or business situation.

4
SUCCESS

Upgrade Your Style and Grooming to Be Seen and Heard as a Winner

YOUR CLOTHES ARE A REFLECTION of the person you are. By the selection of your attire, you control the narrative before you say a word, because what you wear provides the world with a significant amount of information about you. All the world's a stage. What role would you like to play? Dress for it; otherwise, you may not get the part.

The way you dress and groom yourself can not only change the way other people view you, but also the way they listen to what you have to say. When you dress well, people take you more seriously. Coworkers will ask for your input more often and want you on their team; and when it comes to being considered for an opening in your company—assuming you are qualified for the position—you will more than likely be among the first to be interviewed for it. I am certain you have heard the expression, "Dress for the job you want, not the job you have." Projecting a confident, professional image instantly signals you are right for a position.

When you dress well, people take you more seriously.

Dressing well is also an important part of being a gentleman; and more and more men are beginning to realize the importance of their appearance in their social life. This is due in part to the realization that one's image matters a great deal. Dressing well will open doors for you. It can change your life. Dressing well isn't just a confidence booster, it's a personal choice—a lifestyle that helps like-minded people come together—whether it be through social media or in person.

While some men may resent having to conform to specified dress codes, many appreciate knowing how they will be expected to dress. It is considered a gift to them. Richard Thompson Ford, author of *Dress Codes*, writes: "Explicit dress codes can benefit individuals and promote equality by providing clear advance notice of expectations. While an explicit dress code demands only simple adherence, its absence leaves one adrift, forced to navigate ineffable standards of taste, elegance and style—many vague and unwritten or overdetermined and contested."

Rules to follow to be a well-dressed, well-groomed man:

- **Maintain a professional image.**
  Although casual clothes may be the norm for your profession or company, casual does not mean sloppy; it deserves the same attention to detail as a traditional corporate wardrobe. And even with the desire for working professionals to dress more comfortably today, in their fit, brand, and style, clothes still need to signal you take your work seriously. As image expert Eve Michaels says, "Comfort and style are not enemies." It is possible to dress casually as well as comfortably, and still be stylish.

Comfort and style are not enemies.

Dressing professionally in the workplace gives you credibility and shows that you fit in with the work environment. By dressing appropriately for meetings, whether it be in the office or via Zoom video calls, you project a professional image and understanding of the business culture.

- **Look like you care how you look.**
 "Carelessness seems to signal that you don't respect your co-workers or yourself," says Sylvia Ann Hewlett, author of *Executive Presence*. "You certainly don't respect the client if you show up with soup on your tie or bitten nails, anything to make you look unkempt." Clothing should be clean, wrinkle-free, and without holes or frayed areas. Whether you wear suits and tailored clothing or casual attire, your clothes will last longer and look better with some special care.

- **Pay attention to the fit of your clothing.**
 It doesn't matter how much you spend on an article of clothing if it does not fit you properly. Most men's stores and department stores with men's departments have tailors in-house. If you buy something online, you will need to go to a tailor. Many dry cleaners have a tailor or seamstress on the premises.

- **Spend time on your grooming.**
 Poor grooming compromises the ability of other people to see you as someone who is going places because it says that either you don't notice sloppiness, or you don't care enough to attend to it. Immaculate grooming, on the other hand, signals attention to detail.

- **Tailor your look to the situation.**
 When you go for an interview, it's always advisable to dress like the people who work there so they will see you as one of them. "If it's Microsoft, it's one outfit; in the US Army, it's another," says longtime executive recruiter Russell Reynolds. "You have to look like you belong to the group, and you have to look a little better than the group." To do that, pattern yourself after someone who's particularly good at dressing a bit better than the rest of the group.

- **Be selective for a successful image.**
  Select attire that complements your coloring and body type; choose the right clothing and accessories for your business look; adopt meticulous grooming habits, including your hair styling; and build a coordinated wardrobe that combines proper fit and quality construction.

- **Look the part by dressing to the level you aspire.**
  For executive-level, professional, white-collar industries, appropriate business attire consists of quality fabrics and conservative styling in subdued colors. For executive-level positions in fashion-related industries, quality fabrics are also important, but there is more flexibility with styling and color. Technology firms tend to be more casual in their dress than most industries, but there are nevertheless certain standards to be maintained. As you are making your way up the ladder, look like you belong on the level above your current one.

- **Dress for your client.**
  As a general rule, always dress for your client. If you are meeting with an older, more traditional client, for example, and he always wears a suit and tie, you should wear a suit and tie when you meet with him. If you are meeting with a more casual, younger client in the tech industry, you can leave your tie at home. Keep in mind you are not only making a statement about yourself by the way you dress, but also about the company you represent. Does your attire accurately represent your brand?

- **Follow the +1/-1 rule.**
  Sylvie Di Giusto, author of *The Image of Leadership*, recommends dressing one level higher than your current professional level, but not two levels up because you will look overdressed. And, "Never dress down more than one level because you want to dress like the leader you want to be. If you follow the +1/-1 rule you never risk being underdressed or overdressed."

5

SUCCESS

Be Fashion Conscious and Observe Dress Codes

"Fashion is instant language."
—Miuccia Prada

BEING FASHION CONSCIOUS DOES NOT mean you are superficial or even trendy. Fashion can be fun and sometimes seem a bit superficial, depending upon the attire, but it is serious business. Being fashion conscious means you're aware of the message your clothing sends and how important it is to choose the correct attire for the office, occasion, and your social life outside of the office. And it enables you to choose the style of clothing that best reflects your personality, physique, and profession.

Fashion is serious business.

Every man's wardrobe should consist of some basic, essential items in the best quality you can afford. If you buy good quality suits, blazers and coats in conservative styling, you will be able to wear them for many years. When it comes to accessories, this is where quality is extremely important. Shoes speak volumes; and as with clothing, if you buy good quality leather shoes, they will last a long time. Even with traditional or conservative clothing styles, however, there can be variances in the cut from time to time that can make them appear dated. Beware of looking dated, since a dated appearance signals dated skills. Whether it is an accurate observation or not, perception is reality.

The essential wardrobe basics:

- **Suits.** Navy blue, charcoal gray, and black are the colors for the professional white-collar working world, with navy blue and charcoal gray being preferable for investment banking professionals. Even if you do not have to wear a suit to work every day, you should have these suits; they are the essentials. A black suit, for instance, will also be needed for formal affairs. You may also want to have a tuxedo if you often attend events for which black tie is the requested attire. If you live in the South or a warm climate, you may want to add a tan suit to your collection, keeping in mind it is a less formal color for a suit.

- **Jackets/blazers.** Invest in few good ones that you can wear with slacks, jeans, over sweaters, et cetera. You can go with patterned or solid depending on your style. A navy blazer is a must. A black blazer can dress up jeans. And a plaid blazer is a nice change for weekends and casual days at the office.

- **Pants/Slacks.** When buying pants for the office, it is advisable to buy simple, good quality ones in neutral colors, since they will get a lot of wear. Plain, flat-front pants look more sophisticated and more slimming than pleated ones. If you are not wearing a suit every day, these will be your staples most days of the week. The most versatile color is charcoal gray. You can and should change your shirt every day, but it isn't absolutely necessary when it comes to your pants. Dress pants should have a little break, covering the entire back of your shoe but not your heel. With casual pants, your pants should cover the top of your shoe when you are standing. Your pants should fit comfortably on your waist, and preferably have a plain flat front flap. By all means avoid wearing pants that are too tight or have a rise that is too short.

- **Shirts.** You should have at least five dress shirts, one for every working day in a week. A few white ones and a few pale blue ones if you work in the white-collar professional world. You can also include one or two black shirts for evening, or if you work in a fashion or art-related field. If you like patterned shirts, start with stripes; they are more businesslike than those with checks. If you prefer checks, go for a gingham check. Long-sleeved shirts are preferred over short sleeves. Even if you live in a warm climate, rolled-up sleeves look more classic than shirts with short sleeves. Also, when you can afford to, buy a few custom dress shirts to signal you've arrived. Dress shirts should be close fitting, but never so tight that the buttons strain to close.

  Sleeves should reach the break of the wrist and extend by ½ to ¾ of an inch, just showing a bit of the cuff if you are wearing a jacket. Shirt collars should button comfortably without pinching or leaving a gap. And with shirt collars there are a number of styles to choose to go with various face shapes. Be sure to choose the one that's right for yours.

- **Ties/pocket squares.** You should have a few solid color silk ties and a couple of classic rep ties. Start with the Ralph Lauren brand for ties. You can't go wrong; they are always tasteful. Keep in mind: blue is a "trust me" color, red is a power color. Your tie should be long enough to come to the middle of your belt buckle. Also buy a few pocket squares in silk and linen, as well as traditional white cotton ones. When coordinating your pocket square and tie, make sure they are not from the same material or same pattern. Pocket squares should coordinate with ties—never be an exact match.

- **Shoes.** Buy a pair of black, tan, and possibly brown leather shoes to start. Your shoes should be made of real leather with leather soles. When starting out, you can buy a pair of classic black oxford lace-ups and a pair of brown wing tips—sometimes called a "brogue"; derbies with a cap toe for your professional attire; and loafers and Chelsea boots for your casual attire. After that you can extend your collection. Buy the best you can afford and keep them in good condition, resoling and reheeling when they get worn down. Wear black with black, blue, or gray suits; brown looks good with a gray pinstripe suit; and dark brown or tan can be work with tan suits. Tan also works well with a navy blazer and khaki or gray slacks. (By the way, shoes are the first thing a woman looks at.)

- **Jewelry.** For men, jewelry should be kept to a minimum. A watch, wedding ring, tie bar, and cuff links are all the jewelry items a man should wear in a professional setting. Neck chains should be kept under a shirt collar.

- **Belts.** Buy the same color belts as you do shoes, since your belt and shoes should always match. And like your shoes, your belt should be in good condition. At the very least, you will want a dress belt in black leather and a tan or brown leather belt for your more casual attire.

- **Socks.** Your socks should be darker than your dress slacks for suits and formal wear. When in doubt about the color, match your sock color to your shoes—not your slacks. Be sure to buy executive socks, which are high enough to prevent any skin from showing if you cross your legs. When wearing less formal attire, you can have a little fun with your socks and buy colors and patterns, depending on your personality, workplace, and the situation. It's time for new socks when the heels become threadbare.

- **Straight-leg dark jeans.** You can wear jeans with your shirts, suit jackets, black shoes, sneakers, whatever. Everything goes with jeans. Dark jeans are "dress" jeans; lighter blue jeans are more casual. And they can be a bit longer than your suit trousers.

- **White T-shirts.** Crew necks are good to wear under V-neck sweaters. They are inexpensive and versatile. They may also be worn under dress shirts, although V-neck T-shirts are preferable and more modern. T-shirts protect your good shirts from sweat and undue wear and tear.

- **Sweaters.** Gray or black sweaters go well with jeans, suit trousers, or a jacket. Invest in quality wool or cashmere. Cheap sweaters are likely to shrink after a few washes. Also consider buying sweaters in flattering colors to wear on weekends or casual work days.

- **Coats.** As with suits and sweaters, go for quality. A good coat will serve you for years. Optional styles include a classic look, a pea coat, or a duffle coat A trench coat may also be practical, depending upon your location.

6
SUCCESS

The Importance of Confident Body Language

Unless the audience sees the right image, it doesn't hear the right message. We believe it when we see it.
—Mark Bowden, *Winning Body Language*

YOU CAN DRESS THE PART and say the right words—and granted these are extremely important—but if your bearing doesn't match or isn't in harmony with your visual and verbal message, you will not be credible. In other words, you will not be able to successfully communicate your message, since people believe what they see.

From the moment you enter a room, your body is communicating to others who you are, how you feel about them, and how you feel about the situation or event. Body language is the fastest way you can convey confidence and power and exude a winning first impression. Why is confidence so important? Because people are constantly looking for winners to lead them. According to a major study done by Carnegie Mellon, a professional's confidence is more important than a professional's reputation, skill set, or history. An individual who exudes a powerful persona is perceived to be able to affect the world around them. And just like we want our leaders to be confident, we want them to be powerful so that they will be a be able to deliver what they promise.

Presence is significant because it is authentic. It comes from someone believing in their own story and competence. "Presence is the state of being attuned to and able to comfortably express our true thoughts, feelings, values, and potential. Through self-nudges, small tweaks in our body language and mindsets, we can achieve presence," writes Amy Cuddy in *Presence*.

> *Our bodies can change our mind then our behavior and ultimately the results.*
> — Amy Cuddy

Communicate Confidence and Presence with Powerful Body Language:

- **Stand like a winner.**
  Good posture instantly identifies you as someone with something to contribute, and signals you are a confident person. Not only will you look more confident, you will feel more confident. And keep in mind that if you appear confident, people will think you have something to be confident about. People accept what you project.

  It's also important to maintain good posture when sitting. Slouching or bad posture conveys that you are a slob or not as competent as those who sit straight, according to Dr. Lillian Glass, a body language expert.

- **Keep your head level with your chin positioned parallel to the floor.**
  A level head indicates an assured, candid, capable nature. It might also give your voice fuller tones and make you seem to be looking people straight in the eye. A bowed head, eyes studying the floor, makes you look unsure, vulnerable, passive, and possibly even guilty of something.

- **Walk the walk.**
  From the moment you walk in a room with dignity and easy confidence, you tell people you are someone who matters. Walking well begins with perfect posture. Keep your rib cage high and chin up to add confidence to your walk. Think tall and light, keeping your weight forward on the balls of your feet. Do not settle into each step. Maintain your momentum and walk with a natural, comfortable rhythm. In general, powerful walking is more expansive, with more arm movement and a longer stride.

- **Keep hands visible.**
  Avoid putting your hands in your pockets. It makes you appear uninterested or bored, uncommitted, and sometimes nervous. One hand is okay if the other hand is gesturing. Keeping hands open and palms facing upward indicates openness and honesty, and a willingness to connect with people

- **"Pockets are murderers of rapport."**
  When someone can see your hands, they feel more at ease and more likely to befriend you. When walking into a room or waiting to meet someone, keep your hands out of your pockets," writes Vanessa Van Edwards in her book *Captivate*.

- **Make eye contact.**
  When meeting someone for the first time, it's polite to make eye contact for a few seconds, but it's considered quite rude to make eye contact and stare. Brief contact is considered normal, but outright staring at other people is interpreted as hostile or threatening. Not making eye contact is just as powerful. You might break eye contact and look away to signal to the other person you are ready to end the conversation or are frustrated that the other person is talking too much. Not making eye contact

when you meet someone for the first time is also a sign of low self-esteem or lack of self-confidence.

- **Use facial expressions to reinforce communication.**
Your face is a tool for communicating emotions and feelings, and it is also important for regulating and directing an interaction. As the focal point of conversation, the impact of its expressions is magnified. Once you've started a conversation with another person, your facial expressions help to encourage, or conversely discourage, further interest and interaction. In situations where you want to maximize your authority, you should minimize your animation, since being overly expressive can detract from your credibility. When you appear calm and contained, you look more powerful.

- **Smile warmly.**
Smiling is a powerful and positive nonverbal cue for signaling likeability and friendliness. It is especially important to smile when you are meeting someone, since it signals a sincere interest in meeting them and good will toward them.

    "Smiling has huge consequences for establishing connections. A smile can improve and repair relationships or ease conflict. It's a way of saying to the other person you can be trusted," according to Marianne LaFrance, psychology professor at Yale University.

- **Offer a firm handshake.**
The power of the handshake should never be underestimated; a handshake can produce a high degree of trust within a matter of seconds. In Western culture, the handshake is the only acceptable physical touching when you are meeting someone in business for the first time. If you want to make a positive impression and convey confidence, firmly clasp the other person's

hand when shaking hands. Squeeze until you feel their muscles tighten, then stop.

"Handshaking is a valuable form of nonverbal communication. It is a form of interactive body language that offers insights into how the other person views the world, him or herself, and you. It is a vital, if usually subconscious, part of creating a first impression and sending a parting message," writes Robert E Brown and Dorothea Johnson in "The Power of Handshaking"

- **Create a credible, professional vocal image.**
  Voice is an important part of the nonverbal behaviors and cues that you both send and receive. Most people don't know or understand the nonverbal influence of their voice. Before you meet someone for the first time, more than likely you have spoken to them on the telephone. Thus, the opinions they form of you are based on one thing only—your voice. It is vital, therefore, that you project the correct voice image. Speak with optimal volume, articulate clearly, avoid mumbling, avoid filler words and sloppy words. Sound confident in what you are saying, avoiding excessive apologies and upspeak, which is a rise in intonation at the end of a sentence that makes it end up sounding like a question.

- **Use gestures to reinforce communication.**
  If you want to appear comfortable and unguarded, your gestures need to start talking when you begin to speak. Don't think about your gestures; they should appear natural and reinforce what you are saying. Hand gestures make people listen to you. They make people pay attention to the acoustics of speech, according to Spence Kelly, a professor at Colgate University. Use them sparingly at key moments. When you gesture too much or too expansively, it can be distracting and detract from your message.

7
SUCCESS

Enhance All Your Relationships with Refined Social Graces

SOCIAL GRACES ARE SKILLS USED to politely interact with others in social situations. People with refined social graces are generally more likeable, easy to talk to, and a pleasure to be around. They make an effort to build and maintain relationships in their personal and professional life because they know these are vital to them achieving their life's goals. They know the world does not revolve around them; and that to be successful, they will need the support and encouragement of others.

Adopt these refined social graces to enhance all your relationships:

- **Be interested in others and the world around you.**
  People like people who are interested in them and the world around them—not just in themselves. By showing interest in others and the world around you, it shows that you are not self-absorbed, which will help you create positive impressions wherever you go. And the more well-informed you are, the more likely it is that you will have a conversation topic for each person you meet.

You can make more friends in two months by becoming interested in other people than you can in two years by trying to get other people interested in you.
—Dale Carnegie

- **Be a good listener and ask questions.**
  People like to know they are being heard and that their ideas are appreciated. By being a good listener, you let others know that you value them and what they have to say. Most people do not listen with the intent to understand; they listen with the intent to reply. They're either speaking or preparing to speak. After you ask someone a question, listen to their answer without interrupting or finishing their sentences; and direct your nonverbal, "interested" energy toward them—making eye contact, leaning in, and nonverbally responding to them.

- **Be sincere.**
  Flattery will get you everywhere, but only if it is authentic. People can sense when someone is being inauthentic, and they don't like false sincerity; they value authenticity.

- **Be good natured; have a sense of humor.**
  Try to make the best of situations and don't take yourself too seriously. Show a similar attitude when you first meet someone, seeing where you agree rather than disagree. It will put others at ease around you.

- **Be a team player.**
  "We're all in this together; and let's make it work" is an attitude that is appreciated by everyone—at home and at the office.

- **Be optimistic.**
  People like people who are positive. No one wants to be around someone who is always pessimistic and has a negative attitude

toward life. Having a positive attitude can become a habit, just as always being negative can.

- **Be confident.**
  Confidence is an attractive trait; it will make people want to be around you and follow your lead.

- **Be open and approachable.**
  Smile. Make eye contact. Use body language that says "I am open for business." Just as important as being confident enough to approach others is signaling that you are open to meeting and conversing with people.

- **Be skilled at making small talk.**
  Small talk "breaks the ice"; it puts others at ease and makes them feel comfortable.

- **Be polite.**
  Having good manners and a respectful attitude toward others will make people want to be around you—in and out of the office.

8

SUCCESS

Create a Positive, First-Class Vocal Image

THE WAY YOU SPEAK IS considered as or more important than your experience, intelligence, education, appearance, or personality, according to research. Your voice accounts for nearly 40 percent of your first impression and, therefore, carries a lot of weight in how you are perceived. Your speech conveys your mood, authority, level of intelligence, education, and sense of purpose. The minute someone hears you speak they form opinions about you.

Having a positive, first-class vocal image and being a skilled speaker are essential for success in the business world. A negative vocal image can hold you back at your current job, or even prevent you from landing a job you know you are more than qualified for. It is very clear that the sound of your voice and how you use it can either help or hurt your career opportunities.

Convey confidence and credibility with a first-class vocal image:

- **Speak with optimal volume to convey confidence.**
  How loudly you speak is often an indicator of how comfortable you feel. In general, the stronger the volume, the more confident and authoritative you come across. The softer the volume, the softer or weaker you seem.

- **Articulate clearly.**
  Articulation is the process of using the lips, tongue, teeth, and jaw to produce the sounds of speech—the consonants and vowels. In general, the more crisply you enunciate your words, the more intelligent and the more attentive to detail you'll sound. The more lazily you articulate your words, the less intelligent and less credible others will perceive you.

- **Keep your pacing relaxed.**
  When you speak more slowly, you come across more confident and authoritative. Conversely, the more quickly you speak, the less confident you seem. A fast pace is often associated with an infusion of adrenalin, so a person who speaks quickly can appear to be nervous. Slowing down will do many positive things for your image. You will appear more in control, and your audience will have more time to digest the message. Do keep in mind, however, that pacing can vary by geographical region, such as in the South where people often speak more slowly than those in the Northeast.

- **Know when to pause.**
  People who pause more in their conversations come across as more intelligent and better prepared. Pausing shows you have command of the conversation. One way to practice pausing is to add a two-second pause at the end of each thought. Pausing also gives your listener a chance to contribute to the conversation, or to ask questions when you are in a meeting or making a presentation.

- **Highlight your message with expression.**
  Vocal expression brings your conversation to life; and the more expression in your voice, the more personable and engaging you come across. Using tools such as pitch, pace, inflection, emphasis, and emotional range, you "translate" your message for listeners. Ideally, you will avoid speaking when you are unhappy or upset about something, unless it is a personal conversation.

- **Project an upbeat, cheerful tone of voice.**
  Happy is not only a state of being, it's an attitude that will show up in your voice. The smile on your face as you pick up the phone will "show up" on the other end.

- **Avoid using filler words.**
  Filler words include: uh, um, you know, kind of, actually, basically, I mean, right, okay, like. Don't use them; they are considered derailers, and they undermine your credibility.

- **Avoid sloppy words.**
  Sloppy words are words like hmm, eh, nah, yeah, huh. Steer clear of them if you want to be viewed as an articulate person.

- **Avoid self-commenting and apologies.**
  Don't comment on your performance or mistakes in front of others. It makes you appear too self-conscious, focused on yourself rather than your audience. Saying "I'm sorry" one or two times is enough. After that it's excessive.

- **Use thoughtful and considerate words.**
  Words like "please" and "thank you" mean a lot in both your professional and personal life. Take some time to think about and work on your vocabulary.

Dating and Your Voice

"Couples research has shown that listeners are more likely to judge you more physically attractive when you speak in a pleasant tone of voice," writes David Givens in his book *Love Signals*. When speaking with someone you like, your voice should sound softer, warmer, and more caring than when speaking to friends or business associates.

9

SUCCESS

Take Charge of your Attitude

Attitude is a little thing that makes a big difference.
—Winston Churchill

YOUR STYLE OF CONNECTING WITH others, your way of communicating, your respect for others, and your behavior toward others are all reflections of your attitude. Your attitude and your professional image help form the first impression others have of you. Decide what you want, and strive for it with a winner's attitude and positive outlook. Have the confidence to expect acceptance from others and chances are you will achieve it, because people who are focused and positive tend to get what they want.

- **Your attitude forms on the inside and is revealed on the outside.** Your mind and body work together. Each affects the other. When you are happy, you look happy, you sound happy, and you use happy language. Your attitude becomes evident to others by your body language, how you complete your tasks, your attention to details, your consideration of those around you, how you take care of yourself, and in your general approach to life.

- **Your attitude is yours to select and manage.** When you're required to interact with someone you're not interested in, think about the benefits of making a positive connection with that person. If you must attend an event even though you would rather not go, consider the benefits to your career and the leads you may obtain there that will help you land new clients. So instead of being rude to the person you didn't want to talk to, adopt a positive attitude that shows you are pleased to connect with him or her. Before you walk in the door at the event you did not want to attend, put a smile on your face to show you are pleased to be there.

- **Your attitude is a means to an end.**
You can adopt the attitude that will best serve your needs.

10

SUCCESS

Step into Life with Confidence

There is a quality that sets some people apart. It is hard to define but easy to recognize. With it, you can take on the world; without it, you live stuck in the starting block of your personality.
—Katty Kay and Claire Shipman, *The Confidence Code*

WHETHER SOMEONE DEMONSTRATES SELF-CONFIDENCE BY being decisive, trying new things, or staying in control when things get difficult, a person with high self-confidence seems to live life with passion and enthusiasm. Certainty about our capabilities gives us the self-confidence to pursue our goals. Other people tend to trust and respect confident individuals, which helps them build even more self-confidence.

Self-confidence comes from knowing yourself better than anyone else and, after taking a long, hard truthful look at yourself, accepting what is there before deciding if there are any changes you would like or need to make. It means having a high enough level of self-esteem to never allow another person to exploit your strengths or weaknesses. You are the only one who should control your destiny.

- **Leaders must exude confidence if they want people to follow them.**
  People are very reluctant to follow an individual who is looking down, shuffling along, and not appearing confident. This is

because people are taking a risk when they follow a leader, and they want to make sure that the leader is self-assured and will lead them in the right direction.

- **Women are drawn to men with confidence.**
  When you appear confident in yourself, it signifies you are capable of taking care of yourself; and if you are able to take of yourself, you will be able to take care of your partner—metaphorically speaking.

- **Confidence doesn't develop overnight.**
  It is a process that begins at birth and continues throughout your life. Confidence is developed by accepting challenges, trying new things, overcoming obstacles, and staying with something until you succeed.

- **Your self-confidence continues to grow.**
  No matter what your self-confidence level is right now, you can probably improve it. But you need to believe in yourself and your capabilities before anyone else will. Keep a mental list of things you have succeeded at in the past; surround yourself with people like yourself who are successful; accept favorable feedback from others; stay positive; and learn how to manage stress.

Empowering tips to help you boost your self-confidence:

- **Learn the rules of etiquette.**
  The rules of etiquette are like a road map through life. When we know we are on the right road, it makes us feel confident that we will successfully arrive at our destination.

- **Follow the Act formula. Here's how:**
  A = Action: Try new things and overcome obstacles. As you do, you will build the confidence you need to succeed.

C = Courage: To act before you have confidence requires courage. You can get courage from people, from books, from other resources, and from creating it within yourself.

T = Target: To assure your success, you must have a clear target to shoot at—a clear picture of what you want to accomplish or acquire.

- **Confidence will attract others to you.**

  Having confidence in yourself is a very attractive quality to possess, until it crosses over to arrogance. People are drawn to, and want to follow, confident people. They are not drawn to those who are arrogant or conceited. When you have a healthy level of confidence, employers are more likely to trust you with a project, knowing that you will be good at motivating others.

- **Define your personal brand.**

  When a person exudes confidence, we want to work for them, and we are more likely to follow their lead. William Arruda, a personal branding expert, says confidence is important because it is the most attractive brand attribute. "Confidence is the number one byproduct of the personal branding process, because in branding you uncover what makes you exceptional and use it to make career choices and deliver outstanding value."

- **Know your material.**

  Practice makes perfect. Practice builds confidence. The more you practice a speech, a toast, a presentation, the more confident you will be that it will be positively received. Confidence comes from truly knowing your material.

11

SUCCESS

Build Rapport to Connect with Others

You have no credibility if you don't apply mirroring and matching skills to your communication. Mirroring and matching communicates a level of understanding and empathy of that person's world. It is our job as professionals to project that we understand someone's business by tailoring your communication accordingly.

—Page Haviland, Ph.D.

- Rapport is the ability to connect with another person in a way that makes each of you feel comfortable. It involves being able to see eye to eye with them and connect with them on their wave length.
- Being able to create instant chemistry, or rapport, with other people will impact your success when asking for a favor, making a sale, or encouraging conversation with someone new. In fact, up to 90 percent of your success in selling depends on your ability to establish rapport with a prospective customer, according to Janine Driver, body language expert. Business is about building relationships. People do business with people they like and feel comfortable with.
- You have a natural rapport with people with whom you have something in common. You can, however, create an almost

immediate rapport, or at least speed up the process, with someone you have just met by making a concentrated effort to do so.

Ways to connect by building instant rapport:

- **Ask open-ended questions and listen more than you talk.**
  Take a genuine interest in getting to know what is important to another person. Start to understand them first by asking polite questions, but avoid questions designed to discover their secrets or past mistakes. The only way to find out what you have in common is to allow them to tell you about themselves. Empathic listening gets inside another person's frame of reference. You see the world the way he or she sees it, you understand how he or she feels. This does not mean you agree necessarily, simply that you understand his or her point of view.

- **Pick up on key words, favorite phrases, and ways of speaking that someone uses, and build them subtly into your own conversation.**
  It will make the other person feel understood and that the two of you are on the same wavelength.

- **Notice how someone likes to handle conversation—lots of detail or big picture.**
  A big-picture person will become quickly frustrated by someone giving them long-drawn-out details about a subject or project.

- **Use the person's name in conversation.**
  Dale Carnegie said "A person's name is to him or her the sweetest sound." Say the name of the person you are conversing with once every ten to fifteen minutes. Do not say their name more than that or it will look like you are trying too hard.

- **Breathe in unison – a mirroring technique.**
  Aim for a similar level of energy, intensity, and enthusiasm. An

overly enthusiastic person will be out of sync with a more reserved person.

- **Adopt a similar stance – another mirroring technique.**
  Closely match your body language, gestures, voice tone and speed of speaking to the other person's. When we see ourselves reflected in another person—either consciously or subconsciously—we feel connected to them. It makes us trust them and develop feelings of empathy for them. Mimic cautiously, however, otherwise the person may think you are a little strange, or perhaps making fun of them.

- **Treat everyone with respect.**
  Meet others on their level; don't look or talk down to them. Respect their time, energy, favorite people and money.

- **Dress in a similar manner.**
  We automatically like people who look like us. "Birds of a feather flock together." It is why we are always advised to show up for a job interview appearing as if we already work there; in other words, wearing the same or similar attire as the people who work at the company.

12

SUCCESS

Be Charming to Be More Likeable

CHARISMATIC PEOPLE IN GENERAL ARE very charming, attractive people with a remarkable rapport-building ability. They light up a room when they enter it. They have a magnetic personality that attracts others to them, making those entering their sphere feel very special.

Leaders who are charismatic are more likeable and more easily able to earn the trust of their team members, especially if they show them the respect they deserve. And when people feel respected by their leaders and are comfortable with them, they perform better on teams. Additionally, research shows that leaders who rank high in likeability also rank the highest for leadership effectiveness; and that likeability is a must for effective leadership.

The greatest tool charismatic people use to make them more likeable is charm. According to Brian Tracy, "Charm is the ability to create extraordinary rapport that makes others feel exceptional." It is the power of pleasing or attracting others through our personality or beauty. It's the art of letting someone know that you feel good about them without asking anything in return."

> *Charm is the ability to create extraordinary rapport that makes others feel exceptional.*
>
> —Brian Tracy

Becoming a more charming person can advance your career in ways that education, technical skills, and intelligence alone cannot. And it can greatly expand your social circle. While some people seem to have an abundance of natural charm, it is an ability almost anyone can develop with practice. As with any endeavor, the more you practice, the better you become.

Turn on the charm with these strategies:

- **Be genuinely interested in people.**
  Charming people are more interested in what the other person has to say than what they themselves have to say. Encourage others to talk about themselves and their interests.

- **Be a good listener.**
  Give others your undivided attention. Focus on what they are saying, follow up with clarifying questions, and never interrupt them.

- **Foster good conversation.**
  Charming people are exceptional at the conversation skills that lead to meaningful relationships. They know how to begin a conversation, keep it going and graciously end it.

- **Remember names.**
  When you remember someone's name, it shows respect and thoughtfulness; and that you care enough about the person to remember their name.

- **Make eye contact and smile.**
  Eye contact is charm's friend. Remember to look into someone's eyes when speaking to them. Add a warm smile to send a clear message about your state of mind. Research shows that if you look at someone and then smile, it instantly charms them. And,

if you maintain eye contact for a few seconds at the end of your interaction it will make the other person feel truly listened to.

- **Offer genuine compliments.**
  Being charming includes complimenting people. Most people prefer to be complimented on a personality trait or an accomplishment rather than on their appearance—unless it's a date, of course. At the office, complimenting an accomplishment would be the most professional.

- **Make the person feel important.**
  A charming person makes the other person feel as if they are the most important person in the room when they are with them. But you must be sincere in order to be believable.

- **Exude confidence.**
  Erect posture, eye contact, a firm handshake, being dressed appropriately, and being well-groomed will help you exude confidence and make you appear more attractive to others.

- **Be positive.**
  Charming people are known for elevating others—making them feel better after interacting with them. Charm is not only light and fun, it's a powerful tool in interpersonal relationships.

- **Be considerate.**
  It's about the other person, not you. Don't ask for anything in return. Treat people the way you would like to be treated and that consideration will be returned to you in kind. Likable people know this—that's part of what makes them so likable.

13

SUCCESS

Recognize and Manage Emotions with Your EQ Skills

The rules for work are changing. We're being judged by a new yardstick: not just how smart we are, or by our training and expertise, but also by how well we handle ourselves and others.
— Daniel Goleman, *Emotional Intelligence*

THE DICTIONARY DEFINES EMOTIONAL INTELLIGENCE (EQ) as the capacity to be aware of, control, and express one's emotions, and to handle interpersonal relationships judiciously and empathetically. EQ is an extremely important tool for personal and professional success. In fact, it is so important that it is considered even more of a contributing factor to a person's success than their intelligence or technical training and knowledge. Additionally, studies have shown that people with high EQ have better mental health, job performance, and leadership skills. A leader's ability to manage people and relationships is very important, since leaders are not competing with products and services alone but how well they manage their people.

Daniel Goleman, American psychologist and author of *Emotional Intelligence*, developed a framework of the five elements that define people with emotional intelligence. These individuals are very self-aware; able to control their emotions and impulses; highly motivated; empathic;

and have strong social skills. Although these qualities are innate, they can also be learned and refined with practiced effort and experience in successfully dealing with challenges and situations that require the application of these skills.

Conflict resolution boils down to preventing a situation from getting worse, smoothing egos to avoid a buildup of resentment, and reaching agreement on how to move forward to get things done. For these situations in particular, applying your honed EQ skills will enable you to productively solve them with a win-win resolution for all.

Managing yourself with a highly developed EQ:

- **Practice self-awareness.**
  Everyone has doubts about themselves every now and then, but those with EQ doubt themselves less often; and when they do, they confront their issues and deal with them head-on, resolving them in an unemotional, pragmatic manner. The idea is not to abolish your emotions or ignore them, but to be able to recognize them, and effectively deal with them.

- **Acknowledge your emotional reactions and how you feel about the experiences you have each day.**
  Take some time each day to reflect on your experiences and how you reacted to them and, upon reflection, how you might have handled certain ones differently. This is not the time, however, to overthink each experience and begin to doubt yourself. It is the time to learn from your experiences, not judge your emotions.

- **Practice self-control.**
  Don't overreact. Think before you speak or act—particularly if you are feeling emotional about an issue. Think of the long-term effects of your actions or words and not the immediate situation when making consequential decisions.

- **Examine how you react to stressful situations.**
  Is your heart racing? Do you have a knot in your stomach? Are you having trouble breathing? Any of these signs means your emotions are getting out of control. Always pause, collect your thoughts, and, if possible, remove yourself from the situation until you are able to calmly and rationally deal with it.

- **Accept responsibility for your actions.**
  If you have lost your temper or said something you shouldn't have to someone, apologize. Recognizing and accepting the fact that you lost control of your emotions is one of the key factors in taking your EQ skills to a higher level.

Managing others with your highly developed EQ:

- **Be attuned to other people's body language.**
  Often people do not want to voice what they are feeling when distressed; but if you look closely at their body language, you will be able to read the distress signs. Then you can carefully approach them and, with your EQ skills, help them come up with a solution for what is causing them to be distressed.

- **Be empathic and show appreciation for differences.**
  Put yourself in the other person's shoes. Identity, understand, and acknowledge their wants, needs, and differences. The key to appreciating the differences between their view and yours is to realize that all people see the world not as it is, but as they are. Listen empathically but don't try to solve the problem for them. Let them come up with the solution, one that is a win-win for everyone concerned.

- **Be open-minded and listen without judgment or a pre-determined opinion.**
  Openness and being agreeable go hand in hand when it comes to emotional intelligence. A narrow mind is generally an indication

of a lower EQ. When your mind is open through understanding and internal reflection, it becomes easier to deal with conflicts in a calm and self-assured manner.

- **Reassure people; make them feel safe.**
  Employees need to feel they can disclose their feelings and emotions to you and their team members without fear of recrimination or that they will be harshly judged by what they have said. Letting them talk about their feelings and whatever is making them feel anxious or concerned about themselves, their colleagues, or the work culture at the office will help them to be more positively focused on their work

- **Take responsibility for your actions toward others, and try to present a consistent image.**
  If you are in control of your emotions on an ongoing basis, others will know what to expect from you and will feel more comfortable disclosing their negative emotions to you. Being yourself makes being consistent a no-brainer, and other people will trust you more if they understand where you're coming from.

- **Be an active listener, then restate what you heard.**
  Say something like, "If I have understood you correctly, you feel the problem is thus-and-such, and have felt it was so-and-so. Is that correct?" It will be reassuring to the person to know that you truly listened to them and correctly heard what they told you.

- **Ask questions that will clarify, not judge.**
  Asking questions is the best way to understand another human being's actions. But in order to get honest answers, you must know how to ask questions that don't sound judgmental. Asking "why" puts people on the defensive, and defensiveness stops conversation rather than fosters it. Use the words "who," "what," "when," or "how" instead.

14

SUCCESS

Be an Inspirational Leader and Team Builder

Being a leader changes everything. Before you are a leader, success is all about you. It's about your performance. Your contributions. When you become a leader, success is all about growing others. Your success as a leader will come not from what you do but from the reflected glory of your team.

—Jack Welch

AN INDIVIDUAL MAY BE MADE a manager, but not every manager is a leader. One who is, or learns to become one, is an entirely different being. A leader inspires confidence in other people and moves them into action toward achieving a common goal. He or she is part psychologist, part visionary, part motivational speaker, and part persuader, or attitude changer. Inspirational leaders are not born, they are made. Some have had the good fortune to have had an exemplary mentor; others may have taken leadership courses; and still others may have observed their own and others' bosses in the workplace and have adopted the traits of the exemplary leaders.

According to Tom Murphy, who Warren Buffet has said taught him most of what he learned about management, "Much of what you become in life depends on whom you choose to admire and copy. To arrive at leadership greatness, model the leadership of the best managers."

A master plan for becoming an inspirational leader and team builder:

- **Be a leader in your own right.**
  In addition to being in top form with your health and appearance, you need to exhibit executive level presence in order to be credible as a leader. You need to have a reputation as a person with character and integrity. And you need to have an accurate picture of your strengths and weaknesses so that you can build on your strengths and supplement or tackle your weaknesses.

- **Be the kind of leader others want to emulate.**
  To be an inspiration to your team. Lead by example. Make sure your habits and actions match your words. Establish trust and transparency with your team, your superiors and your clients. Be empathic and nonjudgmental.

- **Be present, visible, and transparent.**
  Your team members need to see you on a frequent basis—whether in person or online. When you are at the office, try to find time each day to walk around and check in with your immediate team members. During these informal interactions, be honest and as transparent as possible. This authenticity will build trust between you and your team. It also will lead to stronger relationships and a healthy culture. Furthermore, you will likely find that the time spent observing how your team and business run will help you identify problems and opportunities.

- **Communicate clearly and promptly with your team.**
  Don't keep them guessing. Everyone should be working toward a common goal. It's your responsibility to keep the vision in sight for everyone and ensure that your team members work together to achieve it.

- **Handle your power responsibly and be a mentor to those at the beginning of their careers.**
  You have the fate of those you lead in your hands. Be a benevolent and fair leader, treating people with dignity and respect. Young team members can be especially vulnerable, and the sensitivity shown them, as well as the positive feedback and helpful guidance at the beginning of their careers, can make all the difference in their future success as valuable employees.

- **Set boundaries to build teamwork.**
  Set boundaries by communicating behaviors that are appropriate and as well as inappropriate between superiors and subordinates, and between coworkers, so that you can create a safe environment and a healthy, productive work culture that promotes teamwork.

- **Be a cheerleader for your team.**
  Cheer them on when a job is going well, was well done, and when the team needs encouragement to keep going when the going gets tough. When you and the team show enthusiasm for one another's ideas, joking around and having a little fun allows everyone to feel relaxed and energized.

- **Lead through encouragement rather than criticism and blame.**
  Leadership that focuses on problem solving and encouragement rather than blame will be more successful. Call attention to people's mistakes indirectly and share some stories about times when you might have done a better job. It will make you seem more human and approachable. In personal and business relationships, effectiveness is largely achieved through the cooperative efforts of two or more people.

- **Give praise before giving negative feedback.**
  Recognize talent and express gratitude for top performance and

competence at all levels. Even the boss likes to hear praise. When you do need to give a team member negative feedback, begin with praise for what they've done well first, and let them know you believe whatever needs correcting isn't insurmountable

- **Never embarrass or berate a team member in front of the team or in private.**
  Diplomatically settle disputes with team members in public meetings, and meet privately with individuals who need additional guidance. In personal relationships and businesses, effectiveness is largely achieved through the cooperative efforts of two or more people. A win-lose relationship or solution will not likely accomplish a positive outcome and could lead to resentment by one of the parties.

- **Avoid giving direct orders.**
  Try instead to suggest a solution or ask the team how they would accomplish a task. They'll be more invested and take pride in the outcome if they are involved in solving the problem, and be happier to do what has been proposed.

- **Be a good listener.**
  The best leaders prioritize listening and make sure that they are listening for context as well as content. Additionally, good leaders listen without judgment and without trying to control the conversation. Being a good listener will not only build trust and respect, it will ensure you're getting the correct information you need to make the right decisions.

- **Allow your team members to voice their opinions.**
  In the best teams, members listen to one another and show sensitivity to feelings and needs, according to a Google in-house study. Give your team members an opportunity to share personal stories and emotions. Include everyone. Create a safe environment for people to work and participate.

- **Share the spotlight.**
  Be sure to give credit where credit is due, rather than taking all the credit for a job well done. Confident leaders are never afraid of being upstaged by their team, and when praise is given, they name all who participated in making the project a success.

- **Be mindful of the fact that young employees today are different from those in the past.**
  Today's young people want more fulfillment from their jobs, and they want to work for a higher purpose than money. They want to know work is more than just the hours they spend on the job. And Millennials, in particular, consider feedback very important, so be sure to provide it on a consistent basis—not just when it's review time. These young employees deserve to triumph because they are clear-eyed enough to discard yesterday's conventional wisdoms and how things have always been done by searching out sometimes disruptive, but often more effective, solutions and ways of doing things.

15

SUCCESS

Form Productive Habits and Effective Time Management Skills

> *Successful people have the habit of doing the things failures don't like to do. They don't like doing them either, necessarily, but their disliking is subordinated to the strength of the purpose.*
> —Albert E.N. Gray, *The Common Denominator of Success*

THE HABITS YOU FORM AND how you manage your time play an instrumental role in how successful you will be in achieving your life's goals. Many say time is more precious than money. That is because time is finite, and there are only so many hours in a day. When you have family members and work obligations placing seemingly inordinate demands upon you, it can often seem as if there isn't enough time to meet these demands—let alone have time for the things you would like to do on a more personal level. By forming and maintaining good habits and productive time management skills, you will be able to meet the demands placed upon you and your time.

Habits

Habits—both good and bad—make us. Habits are powerful! Habits are not easy to form and maintain and they take hard work and conscious effort over time to create. You may have read it takes 21 days to form a habit. New research shows it can actually take 66 days on average to form a habit. For some it can take as long as 254 days! The good news is that, as with a bad habit, once a good habit is formed, it is not easy to break. All one needs to do is spend the time it takes to replace a habit that is keeping you from achieving a goal with one that would be more beneficial to you.

Forming good habits is a critical ingredient in leadership. Leaders need to be in control of themselves in order to maintain the repetition of behaviors long enough for habit formation. Possessing evolved emotional intelligence (EQ) will enable you to develop and maintain the strong, defined habits necessary for self-management.

The formation of good habits is also a critical ingredient in achieving happiness and satisfaction in your personal life. It often helps to join forces with someone who shares the same goal and work on it together. Or you can hire a coach to work with you. Or in the case of difficult-to-break, harmful habits, a therapist might be in order. Goals will help you stay on course and ensure you get where you're going in the shortest amount of time. It is only with the strict adherence to your habits, however, that you will achieve your goals.

According to Stephen R. Covey, author of *The Seven Habits of Highly Successful People®*, "Habits are patterns of behavior comprised of three overlapping components: knowledge, desire, and skill. Because these habits are learned rather than inherited, our habits constitute our second nature, not our first. Habits of effectiveness can be learned; habits of ineffectiveness unlearned. Successful people build habits of effectiveness into their daily lives."

I encourage you to read or listen to *The Seven Habits of Highly Successful People®*. It will change your life if you commit yourself to following them. The seven habits are: 1) Be proactive. 2) Begin with the end in mind. 3) Put first things first. 4) Think win-win. 5) Seek first to understand, then to be understood. 6) Synergize. 7) Sharpen the saw.

I listened to this book a number of years ago and it has helped me tremendously. I imagine many of the twenty-five million other people who have bought his book would say the same.

Habits of effectiveness can be learned; habits of ineffectiveness unlearned.
—Stephen R. Covey

Time Management

As Warren Buffet says, "You've gotta keep control of your time, and you can't unless you say no. You can't let other people set your agenda in life." Furthermore, "Really successful people say no to almost everything." When you are at the beginning of your career, your days are not totally under your control, and you certainly cannot say no to your boss when he asks you to do something. You do, however, have a modicum of control over how you allocate your time to these tasks.

Leaders have long to-do lists every day, and it's easy to get diverted from the most important items on those lists. Without good time management skills, leaders can find themselves constantly reacting to issues that arise in the moment rather focusing on the tasks that matter most. To avoid this common problem, you as a leader need to be proactive about time management. Doing so will ensure these tasks don't fall through the cracks, that you're focused on the right priorities, that you're modeling good habits, and that you're meeting all commitments. While time management can be difficult, it is a constructive habit that can be developed.

The question I ask myself every day is, "Am I doing the most important thing I could be doing?"
—Mark Zuckerberg

Strategies for boosting your time management skills:

- **Plan your next day the night before.**
  Spend a few minutes every evening prioritizing and scheduling the next day's tasks. Once the day starts, things can quickly get chaotic and it can be difficult to allocate time properly. You may get certain things accomplished, but you will not be organized

and may find yourself wastefully focusing on tasks or details that do not make a difference for your big picture. Planning what you need to do the night before sets you up to start your day in an organized flow, allowing you to get more done in less time.

- **Get to work early.**
  One of the habits many good leaders possess is being the first, or among the first, in the office every day. Getting in early gives you time to organize your thoughts, handle a few routine tasks, and respond to emails before everyone comes in. Additionally, it sets the right tone for your team and lets them know that you're present, committed, and working as hard or harder than they are. Even if you're working remotely, getting to your desk early will give you extra time to get a head start on the day, address any last-minute changes, and continue to maintain the habit of being early wherever you're working.

- **Don't get distracted: Keep your goals in front of you.**
  Don't let others keep you from achieving the goals or tasks for the day. Making it a habit to have your goals in front of you is the key to increasing your capacity to succeed. Consistently refresh goals in your mind as a way to ensure you're on the right path to achieving them. If you don't employ such a practice, it's too easy to lose sight of what you're aiming for. Instead of leading your life, you find that you're merely reacting to whatever comes up next. When it's your habit to meditate on your goals, you work towards them and achieve them more effortlessly. Accomplishing goals in this way feels incredible; it makes succeeding enjoyable and motivates you to continue to thrive.

- **Delegate whenever possible.**
  Effective time managers are able to determine which tasks require their attention and which ones can be delegated. Delegating is essential for time management because it ensures that leaders

are focused on the right tasks and strategically allocating their time. It also shows your faith in your team when you delegate tasks to them.

- **Plan for focused periods of work time.**
  Leaders are usually good multitaskers as they have to juggle many different responsibilities. But while multitasking is important, it's not always a good thing. Difficult and demanding tasks require periods of focused concentration, so it's important to schedule your time so that each task gets the focused attention it deserves. For such tasks, getting out of the office and working where you will not be disturbed may be called for.

- **Schedule the hardest tasks or ones you least enjoy early in the day.**
  It can be tempting to put off difficult projects, but it's best to schedule the most challenging things on your to-do list early in the day when you have the most energy and focus. Getting these tasks done early ensures they don't serve as a distraction throughout the day. And it will feel good putting them behind you.

- **Learn to say "No."**
  According to Warren Buffet, effective, productive people say no more often than they say yes.

16

SUCCESS

Define Your Personal Brand to Discover What Makes You Unique

Your gifts lie in the place where your values, passions and strengths meet. Discovering that place is the first step toward sculpting your masterpiece, Your Life.

—Michelangelo

PERSONAL BRANDING IS BY DEFINITION the process by which we market ourselves to others. "With personal branding, you are not only thinking about your assets, you are thinking about what you want to be known for and what people seek you out for. Your personal brand is also aligning the image people have of you to where you are headed," according to Meg Guiseppi, a personal branding expert.

Taking the time to define your personal brand will help you discover what makes you unique. And you are unique. No one is exactly like you, and that is a good thing, because it makes you special. In fact, we are all special in that we each have something uniquely ours we can contribute to the world. Define and value who you are and your confidence will grow, enabling you to be your personal best.

Once you have identified your personal brand, you can write a one or two sentence personal brand statement. This is not a job title nor is it a mission statement. It's a summation of your unique promise of value. Over time, it may change slightly, particularly if you have performed this exercise at the beginning of your career. The person you are innately and the one you've always been since childhood will remain relatively the same.

A brand is a set of values. Values are your beliefs and what makes you, you.
—Donny Deutsch

10 steps to creating your personal brand identity

1. **Look back to your childhood and think about the kind of person you were then—and probably still are.**
   How would your friends describe you? How would your elementary teachers describe you? "Peter was a perfectionist." "Peter was a problem solver." "Peter was a born leader." "Peter only cared about having a good time."

2. **Were you born with an extraordinary gift?**
   How could or would you like to use it? Do you have a beautiful singing voice? Are you artistic? Are you a mathematical genius? It would be a shame not to somehow be able to use your gift in some way.

3. **What are you most passionate about?**
   What do you love to do when you have time? Individuals who follow their passions and are able to turn them into careers are often the happiest and most successful people. Of course, sometimes, what you are passionate about may turn out to be your avocation rather than your vocation if you are unable to support yourself and your family with it.

4. **Define the principles that matter to you.**
   This is especially important, since you will want to work for a company with the same principles. Your personal brand should match or be similar to the corporate brand of the company you

work for. Otherwise, it may not work out long term. It will be a mismatch of values.

5. **Make a list of your hobbies and interests.**
   What do they say about you? Are you an introvert or extrovert? Are you best suited to team or independent work?

6. **Write down the professional skills you currently possess and then write down those you want to develop and highlight that will reflect those values.**

7. **Provide relevant information about you as a person.**
   Your credentials come from your past experience, but they may reveal little about your ability to answer the needs of a potential new employer. Therefore, you need to provide additional relevant information about you as a person. Determine what your top three or four personal attributes are that an employer would find valuable. Are you resourceful? Flexible? Forward-thinking? A visionary? A team player? How have you used these to add value to a company?

8. **Differentiate yourself.**
   Think about what you can offer that no one else does, or, if you are looking for a job, how you would do the job differently to set yourself apart. Do your research and identify the search words people will use to find you, and use them in your message. But avoid being so obscure people can't find you or are unsure about what you are marketing. Whether you are starting a new business, selling a product, or looking for a job, you need to differentiate yourself, your services, and/or your product to outshine the competition.

9. **Follow your instinct.**
   Pay attention to your gut and follow its lead. It will help you know deep down when things are off brand for you. Build an

authentic, honest brand that is consistent both offline and online—particularly in social media, which is a guiding force in the decision-making process.

10. **Work the message.**

Once you create the message you want your personal brand to convey, keep it simple and repeat it often. Advertise it, promote it, and market it. Reinforce it at every opportunity online and offline—on your website, in the blogs you write, in speeches you give, at networking events, and in interviews.

17

SUCCESS

Become an Effective Communicator

First, communication is not so much what you say but rather how you say it. And this you can condition and control. The tone of your voice; your choice and use of words; your inflection, articulation, and delivery; and body language determine how much your listeners take in—and what overall impression of you they will form and retain as a result.
—Sylvia Ann Hewlett, *Executive Presence*

- **Communication skills are some of the most important skills you will need to succeed in the workplace.** Therefore, being able to communicate effectively is essential if you want to build a successful career.

- **Effective communication skills also increase the quality of our lives.** We all have misunderstandings with people who are important to us. It's easy to become confused, frustrated, and disappointed when you are unable to effectively communicate with someone. In order to do so, you need to understand the emotion behind the information or feedback you are receiving, because emotion is the driving force behind the decisions most people make. Being an effective communicator will improve relationships at home, at work, and with your friends, as well as help build trust and respect.

- **Effective communication is more than just exchanging information.** We have to send, receive, and process countless verbal and written communications. In order to be an effective communicator, you must understand your intended message, the audience you are sending it to, and how it will be perceived—from "sender" through to "receiver." And you must be comfortable with the different channels of communication—face-to-face, voice-to-voice, written via email. text, or virtually.

- **You have five message givers: your tone of voice, your eyes, your face, your bearing, and your clothes.** Your audience will be observing your physical movements, posture, gestures, vocal expressions, and eye contact, along with your attire. You need a well-coordinated, congruent message with all five conveying the same message to be believable. Over 90 percent of your message will be communicated non-verbally.

> *If you want to make a positive impression at your next meeting, sales pitch, or job interview, pay attention to what your body is saying. Walk, talk, and look like a leader whom people will want to follow.*
>
> —Carmine Gallo

Actionable tips for effective communications:

- **Presentation: Practice, Passion, Presence.**
  Practice, practice, practice. A well-practiced presentation presented with passion and executive presence is sure to be well-received by your audience, whether you are addressing a few or a few hundred people.

- **Be sure your voice is in optimal condition before making a presentation.**
  An articulate, confident-sounding speaker will be far more credible than a less than articulate speaker who has a hard-to-understand accent, monotone voice, and/or uses too many distracting filler words like um, uh, basically, and you know. If you have a strong accent, you might consider taking accent-reduction classes.

- **Make eye contact.**
  Nothing is more important than establishing and maintaining eye contact with your audience. It is a sign of respect; and it provides you with important feedback on how your message is being received. Do they appear interested? Bored? Confused? When you make eye contact with an individual, maintain it until you finish a sentence or a thought.

- **Be careful choosing your words, and offer to clarify if necessary.**
  Make sure your words represent what you really mean. When you are communicating with someone, you want them to clearly understand your message. If your audience appears to be unsure of your meaning, ask them if they need clarification.

- **Attempt to understand others' perceptions.**
  We all see the world differently. "Seek first to understand, then to be understood." You must speak to the other person's paradigm for them to fully understand your message.

- **Simplify and clarify your message.**
  You are communicating to the overwhelmed and distracted. A direct, simplified message is your best method of communicating in today's world. Good communicators use the KISS (Keep it simple and straightforward) principle. They know less is often more and that good communication should be efficient as well as effective.

- **Talk with, not to, people.**
  If you want to avoid sounding like a college professor, don't lecture your audience. It can make them feel inferior, or that you think they are less intelligent. Engage them in the presentation. It will make them more attentive when they are a participant in the communication process.

- **Repeat, repeat, repeat.**
  Every opportunity you have to communicate your message, repeat it. Some say a message needs to be repeated three times for optimal effectiveness. Others believe the "Rule of 7" applies, meaning consumers need to hear a message seven times before they will consider taking action.

- **Look for metaphors or stories to make your message more memorable.**
  Companies, brands, and persons who take advantage of metaphors will win over audiences every time. It has been proven that people emotionally respond to stories more than facts. Emotion sells. Research shows the most effective way to reach the hearts and minds and move your audience to action is through metaphors and analogy. To capture the attention of your audience right from the start, begin your presentation with a well-honed story to personally connect with them.

In any situation that calls for you to persuade, convince or manage someone or a group of people to do something, the ability to tell a purposeful story will be your secret sauce. Telling to win through purposeful stories is situation, industry, gender, demographic, and psychographic-agnostic. It's an all-purpose, everyone wins tool.
— Peter Guber

- **Be dynamic to connect with your audience.**
  You are the number one visual for your presentation. If you move around the room rather than standing behind a podium, you become more compelling; and as a result, people are more likely to listen to you and remember your message. Avoid showing too many slides—or even any—unless they are mostly images and reinforce your message Otherwise, you will lose your audience midway through the presentation.

PART TWO

Your Guide to the Business World

18

SUCCESS

Thrive in the Business World with Honed Soft Skills

Your education, resume, and technical skills may get you in the door, but your polished soft skills are what will enable you to land jobs, get promotions, win clients, or successfully launch a new business. So, what are soft skills? Soft skills refer to a cluster of personal traits including your work ethic, your personality, your social graces, your attitude, your communication skills, and a host of other personal attributes that are crucial for success in business.

People with first-rate soft skills are most likely to be excellent communicators, team players, masterful at building and maintaining relationships, and able to diplomatically solve disputes. Soft skills enhance an employee's relationships and performance on the job. Individuals who possess well-honed soft skills are highly sought after and valued in the workplace.

Employers are increasingly rewarding workers who have both social and technical skills, rather than technical skills alone; and today's job market favors those who have the skills to interact well with others and be team players," according to a new analysis by David Deming, Harvard education economist. "Jobs where you just sit in a cubicle or on the factory floor and work in isolation are going to disappear," he said. "Workers who combine social and technical skills fare best in the modern economy."

Honed soft skills guaranteed to help you thrive in the business world:

- **Be interested in others and the world around you.**
  People like people who are interested in them and the world around them, not just in themselves. "Your goal is to make others feel comfortable around you by focusing on *them*; and you can influence people's perceptions of you by playing to their needs," writes Camille Lavington in *You've Only Got Three Seconds*. Knowing what's going on in the world will not only make you appear less egocentric, it will also equip you with conversation topics for everyone with whom you come into contact.

- **Be a good listener and ask questions.**
  "Research has consistently demonstrated that ineffective listening habits present the most common barriers to success in relationships and careers," according to Larry Barker and Kittie Watson, authors of *Listen Up*. People like to know they are being heard and that their ideas are appreciated. By being a good listener, you let others know that you value them and what they have to say. Etiquette expert Letitia Baldridge said, "Politeness decrees that you must listen to be kind; intelligence decrees that you must listen to learn."

- **Be skilled at relationship management.**
  "Relationship management is your ability to use your awareness of your own emotions and those of others to manage interactions successfully," according to Travis Bradberry and Jean Greaves, authors of *Emotional Intelligence 2.0*. People like to work with people they like, trust, and feel understand them. Today's workplace can be very stressful; but when you are skilled at relationship management, you can more effectively work with your team members to overcome seemingly insurmountable challenges

and obstacles to achieve a win-win scenario for all, which is what good leaders seek to accomplish.

- **Be good natured and have a sense of humor.**
  Be positive, and try to make the best of situations. A judicious and tasteful sense of humor can often deflate tense situations; and studies show having a sense of humor can help you get ahead at work. A Robert Half survey, for instance, found that 91% of executives believe a sense of humor is important for career advancement, while 84% feel that people with a good sense of humor do a better job. Another study by Bell Leadership Institute found that the two most desirable traits in leaders were a strong work ethic and a good sense of humor.

> *A sense of humor is the art of leadership, of getting along with people, of getting things done.*
> —Dwight D. Eisenhower

- **Be a team player.**
  "We're all in this together, and let's make it work" is an attitude that is appreciated by everyone. According to Harvard professor David Deming in his paper "The Growing Importance of Social Skills in the Labor Market": "As work is becoming more team-oriented, workers with strong soft skills are more able to work well with others and will be considered more valuable, since good teamwork increases productivity." Being on a team often requires flexibility, especially in today's fast-paced work environment. Be ready to shift gears if necessary for the good of the team and project at hand.

- **Be polished.**
  Your appearance remains one of the main factors that will encourage others to work with and for you. It is important, not only in first impressions, but also in ongoing interactions. It is the

filter through which your talent, suitability, and communication skills will be evaluated. According to a research study by senior managers in the U.S., polish is by far the most important aspect of appearance. Polish your appearance for success!

- **Be confident.**
  "Confidence is important because it is the most attractive personal brand attribute. When someone exudes confidence, we want to work with them; we are more likely to follow their lead," says William Arruda, personal branding expert. And, "Employers will know they can trust you with a project and that you are likely going to be good at motivating others as well," according to Dr. Katharine Brooks, author of *You Majored in What? Your Path from Chaos to Career*. If you are in the process of attempting to boost your less-than-ideal level of self-confidence, do as Amy Cuddy advises in *Presence:* "Fake it 'til you become it, until you have reached your optimum level of confidence in yourself."

- **Be an effective communicator.**
  Communication skills are among the most important skills you will need to succeed in the workplace. "First communication is not so much what you say, but rather how you say it. And this you can condition and control," according to Sylvia Ann Hewlett, author of *Executive Presence*. Your words and your body language must be congruent to be believable.

  Furthermore, in order to be an effective communicator, you must understand what your message is, what audience you are sending it to, and how it will be perceived. If is it not perceived the way you intended, you did not effectively communicate your message.

- **Be skilled at making small talk.**
  Small talk "breaks the ice." It makes others feel comfortable and puts them at ease. It is the first level of a conversation; it's about

the current situation, how you got there, the weather, the location, mutual friends or other connections, such as sports, your pets, or your children. When you work in an office environment, making small talk and socializing with team members is essential for building rapport.

- **Be polite and treat everyone with respect.**
  Good manners will be noticed and approved of just as poor manners will always work against you. Having good manners and a respectful attitude toward others will make people want to be around you, in and out of the office.

Civility lifts perceptions of warmth and competence. Civility lifts people.

—Christine Porath

19

SUCCESS

Master the Art of Courteous Greetings and Smooth Introductions

MANY PEOPLE ARE UNCOMFORTABLE MAKING introductions and starting conversations with new people. How many times have you walked up to a group, hoping to be introduced, and been ignored instead? Have you ever gone blank on your best friend's name when it came time to introduce him or her? Have you not known what to say when you were introduced to someone? We have all had these awkward moments; so, since we know how it feels, it should make us want to try harder to graciously navigate these social encounters.

We should always introduce people unknown to each other because it is the polite thing to do. It is comforting to people to be known by their name and to know the names of the people they are surrounded by, as well as to know something about them. To stimulate conversation—a second reason for making introductions—you should include information about each person that can act as a conversation starter.

Knowing how to properly introduce yourself and others and make polite conversation are basic social skills everyone should possess. They will give you an edge and allow you to make a favorable impression right from the start.

I. Introductions

The Rules for Introducing Yourself

A self-introduction is how you make yourself known to another person. Although it's nice to have another person introduce you to people you don't know, sometimes you need to take the initiative and introduce yourself.

It is your duty as a guest at a social event to introduce yourself if your host is occupied with other guests. Do not act shy or reclusive. Your self-introduction should include something that establishes what you have in common with the other people at the event.

> *Getting to know new people and gaining new friends is one of life's greatest pleasures. So, conquer your fears and get out there.*
>
> *—Tony Clark*

- Walk up to a person you would like to meet or a person who is standing near you at an event and smile, extend your hand, and state your name. You may say something like "Hello. We haven't met. My name is Bob Smith."
- If you are seated next to someone at a dinner party or business meal and haven't been introduced, take the initiative and introduce yourself.
- At a business function or event, your self-introduction should include identifying the company at which you work, and possibly your title or function at that company. Example: "Hello, my name is James Madison. I work at Goldman Sachs, helping my clients reach their financial goals."
- You should not use your honorific or title when introducing yourself at a social function. A professional, such as a doctor or judge would, however, use his or her title during the day at work when they are meeting with their patients, et cetera.

15-Second Self-Introduction for Business

A self-introduction is a quick statement about you. It should be concise, compelling and conversational. If you are scheduled to attend an event, you need to have a planned and practiced self-introduction. Tailor your self-introduction to each event. Your self-introduction should include your full name, title, company where you work, something about yourself that establishes what you have in common with the other people at the event, and possibly a call to action, such as "How may I reach you"?

The Rules for Introducing Others

It is important to introduce people in the friendliest, most gracious way possible. Social etiquette is based on respect and courtesy, so both formal and informal introductions are made according to age and gender.

The protocol for business introductions differs from social introductions, since business introductions are based on power and precedence. The name of the most important person is said first, regardless of gender, and he or she gets to know the name of the other person first. As with social introductions, a last name and title should always be given in a formal introduction.

- Always stand for an introduction. If it would be awkward for you to stand, say, "Please excuse me for not standing."
- Use first and last names when you are making a formal introduction.
  Example: "Susan, I would like to introduce Sam Cohen to you. Sam, this is my friend Susan Watkins from New York. Sam is on my team at First Republic."
- There are four age categories for social introductions: seniors or grandparents, middle-age adults, teenagers, and children. Address the oldest person first, regardless of gender, using their title and first and last name. Example: "Bob, I would like to introduce my sister, Sara Jane Hopkins. Sara Jane, Bob Smith is my neighbor in Southampton."

Note: If Sara Jane is much younger than Bob Smith, she would reply using his last name: "Hello Mr. Smith, my brother has told me what a delightful neighbor you are. It's a pleasure to get to meet you."

- In social introductions, address a woman before a man and a girl before a boy.
- If two people are the same gender or same age, it doesn't matter whose name you say first.
- In both the social and business arenas, a VIP or elected official's name is always said first, and their title precedes their last name only. Official persons take precedence over nonofficial persons. Example: "Mayor Abbott, I would like to introduce my husband, Jay Fitzpatrick, to you. He is a big fan of your bike paths in the city. Jay, this is Mayor Abbott, the mayor of Lexington, Kentucky."
- When introducing someone to a group of people, say the new person's name first before giving the names of the others in the group. Look at each person you introduce and talk about each person equally. Or you can just say the new person's name and ask everyone to please introduce themselves to him or her.
- Introductions are based on power and precedence in the business arena. The greater authority's name is spoken first, regardless of gender. Always include the title of each when introducing them. Clients' names are also spoken first, regardless of gender.
- An official person should receive a nonofficial person. This means the nonofficial person is presented to the official person. The most formal way of presenting or introducing the person would be to say, "President Biden, may I present Mr. Robert Davison. He is a supporter of yours from Virginia."
- When you are introduced to someone, you should respond with "Hello" and their name and/or title, accompanied by a smile and handshake. If you are meeting someone older than you, a senior executive, or client, it is always wise to use the person's last name until they give you permission to use their first name. "Hello, Mr. Fitzgerald."

- If you can't remember someone's name when you need to introduce them, extend your hand, smile, and say your name. The other person will then say his or her name. Or if that fails, apologize and let the other person know you can't recall his name. Do mention something you recall about the person. By doing so, you let them know you remember *them*, even if you can't recall their name.
- There are a number of ways to help yourself remember names, but the one I believe works the best is to "associate and anchor." Look at the person's face when you are introduced and tie the name to someone else you know with the same name. It could be a friend, a celebrity, your first pet.
- If someone doesn't remember your name, come to their rescue immediately. Extend your hand, smile, and say your name.
- Avoid making these faux pas: "Have we met before?" or "Do you remember me?" You will either insult or embarrass the other person which, of course, you won't want to do if you have good manners.

II. Global Greetings: Contact and Non-Contact

Regardless of whether you are using a contact or non-contact greeting, you should always stand for greetings and introductions. Once you have stood up, smile and make eye contact with the person as you state your name. If you are the person who is initiating the greeting, you would say something like, "Hello, my name is Ben Sullivan." If you are on the receiving end of the greeting, your response would be something like, "Hello, Ben, I'm John Johnson." Depending on differences in ages, cultural background, or personal preferences, it may be more correct to greet the person you are meeting in a more formal matter, using their last name, rather than their first.

Contact Greetings

- **Greeting with a handshake.**
  As the spoken greeting occurs, the person initiating the greeting should reach forward with his right hand and shake the

other person's hand with a firm grip. Keep in mind, however, that handshakes vary globally. In the U.K., it is a brisk couple of strokes. In Germany, it is a single hand down and back. Be sure to learn the relevant protocol when traveling to foreign lands.

- **Greeting with the Continental "Cheek" Kiss.**
Depending upon the culture, how well you know a person, and the setting, you may be greeted with a kiss. When greeting a client in a business setting, let a client be the first to initiate the less formal "cheek kiss" greeting. The proper procedure is right cheek to right cheek, then left cheek to left cheek, although it can vary by country, such as in Italy, where they begin with the left cheek first.

Non-Contact Greetings

- **Greeting with a bow.**
Although Asian/Eastern cultures are adapting to the Western handshake greeting, if you are traveling to a country where bows are the standard form of greeting, incorporate a slight bow into your greeting. It shows you respect their culture. A handshake, however, is still the greeting of choice in business worldwide.

- **Head nod.**
You can simply lower your head slightly as if you were going to bow as you state your greeting: "Hello, Mr. Johnson. It is a pleasure to meet you." Of course, if you are greeting an Asian business person, you might lower your head a little more, although it is not required if you aren't Asian. It is, however, a sign of respect in the Asian culture.

- **Hand over heart.**
You can put your hand over your heart as you state your greeting. Many cultures associate the gesture with honesty. It indicates that

one is not bearing arms—as does the handshake—or that one appears to have genuine intentions, or is giving one's word of honor. In the United States, of course, we put our hand over our heart when pledging allegiance to the flag.

- **Namaste greeting.**
This is the traditional Indian greeting, which is done by placing your palms together, fingers pointed upwards with thumbs close to the chest, while bowing your head slightly. It is not necessary to say Namaste unless you are Hindu. This is a greeting I have seen a number of world leaders use and I like it because it makes it immediately clear to another person that you will not be hugging, kissing, or shaking their hand.

If you're in doubt as to which greeting to use, I recommend using the one your colleagues are using. If you are a junior executive meeting a senior executive or have a job interview, I recommend deferring to the person you are meeting by adopting their preferred greeting. Another factor to consider is if you are meeting a person from another culture. That's why the handshake is so ideal: it's a universal professional greeting that is never misunderstood

20

SUCCESS

Make Artful Small Talk and Polite Conversation

The goal of the first few minutes of any conversation with someone you don't know is threefold: (1) to find out a few things about the other person; (2) to tell a few things about yourself; and (3) to find some common ground between you.

—Rosalie Maggio, *The Art of Talking to Anyone*

Failsafe pointers for making artful small talk and polite conversation:

- **Begin conversations with small talk.**
  Keep the tone and content of the conversation light until you find a topic you are both interested in. Initial topics are usually about the current environment or situation—how you got there, the weather, the location, mutual friends, or the event you are attending.

- **Ask open-ended questions instead of questions that can be answered with a yes or no.**
  Open-ended questions begin with how, what, where. Be careful about why and when questions, since they put others on

the defensive. Save them until you get to know someone well. A proven ice-breaker question that never fails is "Tell me about yourself."

- **Make your compliments sincere.**
  Paying someone a compliment is one of the easiest ways to start a conversation. Great conversationalists keep the spotlight on the other person and make them feel good about themselves. Should someone pay you a compliment, graciously acknowledge it but don't feel you must reciprocate.

- **Practice active listening skills.**
  Listening is the most important part of a conversation. The best conversations aren't about what you say, they're about what you hear, enabling you to ask clarifying questions and paraphrase back what you heard. Show you are actively listening by making eye contact, nodding, and verbally responding, "Yes, I see, etc."

- **To be interesting, be interested.**
  Show genuine interest in what interests the other person. When you are interested, when you let people talk, they feel pleasure. We remember people who make us feel good.

- **Avoid asking personal questions.**
  Asking someone if they are married, how much money they make, what something costs. how old they are, where they live, or asking any question that seems too probing into their personal life is considered impolite for someone you have just met. Also, avoid mundane questions such as "What do you do?" or "How are you?" These questions are rated the most boring questions one can ask, according to research.

- **Acceptable topics of conversation.**
  Acceptable topics of conversation for someone you have just met

include hobbies and leisure activities, travel, sports, entertainment, cultural events, community involvement, and so forth.

- **Avoid expressing your ideas, attitudes, and opinions with new people.**
  It is wiser to stick to facts rather than getting into what could be controversial territory where you might inadvertently offend or annoy someone you have just met. Eventually, if you are to become friends or have a relationship with someone, you will want to learn more about their personal opinions and attitudes regarding relevant issues; but those discussions are not for a first, brief encounter with someone at a social gathering.

- **Responding to a rude question.**
  If someone asks you a rude question, you are not required to answer it. However, you certainly don't want to show your lack of manners by being rude back; so, for instance, you can respond with this question: "Do you mind telling me why you're asking?" Or you can simply say, "That's personal and I don't like to talk about money" (or whatever it is. You can also ignore the question and change the topic.

- **Identify a common bond or commonality you share with another person.**
  Make an effort to find a few things in common with the other person; and once you find some things in common, the conversation will flow naturally. Try to establish a feeling that you are on the same wavelength. Be agreeable: consider your response before disagreeing. If the point wasn't important, ignore it rather than appearing argumentative.

- **Forget yourself.**
  Use the word "you" more often than you use the word "I," otherwise the person you are talking to will lose interest in the

conversation. Although talking about ourselves gives us pleasure, if we are generous conversationalists, we will give the other person a chance to talk about himself or herself so that they feel pleasure.

- **Take turns.**
  If you have talked for a few minutes without input or comments from your conversational partner, more than likely you were talking too much and not giving him or her a chance to speak. A conversation is an interactive communication between two or more people, which means each person should have an equal chance to contribute to the exchange of thoughts and ideas.

- **Proceed with caution.**
  When a conversation is going smoothly and you feel an instant connection with someone you've just met, you might get carried away and disclose more than you should. If you pause and the other person changes the subject, it probably means you were dominating the conversation or making them feel uncomfortable.

- **Avoid complaining about your problems.**
  No one is really interested in hearing about your problems. Complaining about them is considered the most boring topic of conversation according to research. Everyone has problems, but it shows a lack of interest in the other person to talk about yours.

- **Have something to say.**
  Know a little about a lot of things. Be informed; know what it is going on in the world. Have a few interesting tidbits to insert into the conversation when there's a lull. Did you hear? Did you see?

- **Be tactful.**
  Remember the saying, "If you don't have something nice to say, don't say anything at all." Of course, if someone asks you a

question about how they look, for instance, and you do not think they look good, rather than telling them this, think of something positive to say. Being tactful is part of having good manners.

- **Do not panic over lulls in a conversation.**
  If you feel good about a conversation you're having, a break in it will not feel uncomfortable. A little silence is not necessarily a sign of boredom; but sometimes it does mean it's time to mingle. Don't make yourself and the other person feel uncomfortable by waiting too long to end the conversation.

- **Entering conversations with one, two, or more people.**
  Approaching a person by himself or herself is ideal. The person should—and usually will—welcome you. However, walking up to two people who are in the midst of a conversation is considered intrusive and not recommended. On the other hand, while entering a group conversation can be intimidating, the people in the group should welcome you. When there is a break in the conversation, ease into the group, smile, introduce yourself, and shake hands with everyone. Sometimes it's nice to ask: "May I join you?"

- **End the conversation on a positive note.**
  People always remember how you made them feel, so be sure the last impression you leave with them is as positive as your first impression. It's the conversation's emotional imprint that remains.

5 Simple Steps in the Conversation Process

1. **Begin the conversation.**
   Signal a desire to talk and look for signals from the other person that they would welcome meeting and conversing with you. If you make eye contact with someone and they look away, it's their way of silently telling you they aren't interested in talking to you.

That's okay. There will be someone else who will welcome the opportunity to meet you and get to know you.

2. **Make a statement, then ask a question to engage the other person.**
   "What an impressive selection of wines there is at this tasting event. Which wines do you usually prefer—red or white?"

3. **Introduce yourself.**
   Your self-introduction should include your first and last name at a formal or business event, along with something about you that will help stimulate conversation. "Hello, I'm Jack Sorenson, John's best man and college roommate from Columbia."

4. **Raise a topic.**
   Ask a question and build on earlier comments. If the other person raises a topic you don't like, be ready with an alternative. There are countless topics to raise, just don't be the one asking all the questions. There should be give and take.

5. **Make a gracious exit.**
   When it's time to go, signal the end is near. If there is a reason to contact the person, ask for their business card. If there is no reason to ask for their card or to give them yours, you still need to make a gracious exit. For example, "I have so enjoyed hearing about your trip to Alaska, but if you will please excuse me, I would like to get something to eat (drink)." Or, "It has been great hearing about your new venture. If you would like to give me your contact information, we can schedule time for you to come to the office and tell my team about it." Then exchange business cards.

21

SUCCESS

Mingle with Ease and Grace at Networking and Social Business Functions

Your primary goal when networking and mingling at business functions is to leave people with a favorable impression of you and a desire to know more. The following guide will provide you with everything you need to know to mingle with ease and grace at all your functions, ensuring that you make a positive and memorable impression.

A complete guide for savvy social mingling and networking:

- **Prepare for the event.**
  Prepare as you would for a conference or meeting. Make a list of people who will be attending the event. Set a goal. Visualize yourself circulating, walking up to people, and starting conversations. Be current on the day's news, particularly any recent news pertaining to your field. You may not, by the way, bring this news up in your conversations—especially if a topic is controversial— but you do not want to appear clueless if someone does mention an earthshattering news story.

- **Have a snack before you go.**
  This will give you energy and help you focus on the event and mingling rather than eating. Plus, you don't want to appear to be eager for the food and beverages or have an alcoholic beverage on an empty stomach. And, of course, you will keep your alcoholic beverages to a minimum at a business event.

- **Take your time entering the event.**
  Everyone watches the entrance. Take advantage of this opportunity to create a favorable first impression. Enter, move right or left, and pause for a few seconds instead of rushing into the room. This will also give you a chance to locate your colleagues and the key people with whom you want to engage at the event.

- **Dress appropriately and be well groomed.**
  If you want to be taken seriously, you need to look the part. For most business events, a jacket is recommended. Good breath is a must, as are polished shoes, wrinkle-free clothes, a shaven face, and a fresh shirt.

- **Be sure to speak to the key people at the event.**
  If you are attending a large event, you may not have time to speak to everyone; therefore, you should exchange a few words with the key people before speaking to others. It also sets a good example for your team to see you engaging with clients and C-Suite executives.

- **Acknowledge your peers.**
  Warmly greet your peers and spend a few minutes exchanging pleasantries with them. Do not, however, spend the entire evening with them. If you are a junior staff member, the senior staff members will be observing you to see how savvy you are at mingling. Being skillful at mingling and networking are viewed as

particularly valuable skills to possess for client-based firms that need to attract new clients to grow their businesses.

- **Make a great impression with executive level presence.**
 This means you will maintain erect posture, a warm smile, firm handshake, and direct eye contact. And that you will maintain a formal demeanor, speaking and laughing quietly. If it is a younger, more casual group and the noise level is a little higher, then it would be perfectly fine for you to match the mood of the event.

- **Avoid being pushy, aggressive, or ostentatious.**
 Never get right down to business before building rapport with a person, especially at a social business function. Even if you only have a few minutes to establish rapport, take the time to truly connect with the person in front of you. However, avoid getting overly friendly or flirtatious at a business function. At purely social functions, you can be more flirtatious, but even then, you don't want to make someone feel uncomfortable.

- **Come prepared with a compelling and easy-to-understand self-introduction.**
 One self-introduction does not necessarily fit all occasions. While you do want to have a well-thought-out, consistent self-introduction, it can vary slightly depending upon the particular event. For some events, you may want a more informal way of telling people what you do rather than giving them your formal job title.

- **Always be prepared for a handshake by holding your cocktail utensils in your left hand.**
 Your beverage should be held in your left hand to leave your right hand free for a handshake. Make sure you have a cocktail napkin under your glass so you can dab your fingers before shaking. If

you are carrying a plate of hors d'oeuvres, do so in your left hand as well, with the glass placed on the edge of it when you shake hands. Again, be sure to dab your fingers to avoid shaking a person's hand with food residue on yours.

- **Eating at business events.**
  Take only one canape at a time, avoiding, if possible, anything that requires two bites, or anything that is messy. If you did not have a snack before attending the event, it might be a good idea to have one before you start mingling. Do not, however, rush to the food table as soon as you get there or before you have said hello to the host.

- **Master the art of small talk and making people feel important.**
  Take your time to sincerely focus on each person you meet. Even if you only have a couple of minutes to establish rapport, take the time to really connect with the person in front of you. People will remember how you made them feel more than they will remember what you said, so don't overthink every conversation.

- **Circulate and mingle.**
  Be cognizant of where the best spots are in the room to initiate conversations and where not to approach people. The two worst spots are the entrance and the coat check. After people have checked in and gotten something to drink, they will be more relaxed and ready to circulate. This is the time to gracefully enter or start a conversation.

- **Be mindful of people's time.**
  Parties and networking events are not meant for intense or long conversations. Your primary goal when networking is to leave people with a favorable impression of you and a desire to know more. This means that you spend a few minutes with them to

achieve this goal, but not so much that you are monopolizing them. Allow others a chance to mingle.

- **Don't melt from conversations.**
  Always make a gracious excuse for why you are ending a conversation with someone. Keep in mind, people will always remember how you made them feel, rather than what you said. Before walking away, smile warmly and let them know how much you enjoyed speaking with them.

- **Avoid being a close talker.**
  Respect personal space by maintaining the appropriate distance from others. In the U.S., the appropriate distance between you and another person at a social gathering is from one-and-a-half to four feet.

- **Take business or social cards with you.**
  Business cards may not be appropriate at social functions such as dinner parties; but always take business cards with you to a business function, otherwise, you'll look unprepared. You should wait to be asked for your business card before giving it to someone. It should be in perfect condition and offered to the person with your right hand. And keep in mind that a junior executive should not ask a senior executive or higher authority for his or her card. You should wait for it to be offered to you.

- **Be specific when asking for leads to expand your network.**
  The more specific you are, the more likely it is you will get the appropriate leads. If you happen to be told about an opportunity that might not be right for you but would be perfect for someone you know, be sure to pass it on to them. Networking should be a reciprocal endeavor, or mutually beneficial. It isn't just about you. By helping others, you help yourself.

- **Follow up with people.**
  This will allow others to view you as trustworthy—keeping your word. It's one of the most important traits to possess in business and in your personal life.

- **Always thank the host.**
  Before leaving the event, be sure to thank the person who hosted it. And the next day you may want to follow up with a handwritten or emailed note of thanks.

22

[SUCCESS]

Formal Onsite Business Meeting Protocol

When formal business meeting protocol is followed, it establishes respect among meeting participants, helps meetings begin and end on time, and promotes an atmosphere of cooperation. A lack of adherence to the protocol and poor planning are two of the main reasons why many business meetings fail.

Most executives—at all levels—find meetings are often more of an annoyance than helpful. Nevertheless, there are times when they must be held to foster a spirit of cooperation among all levels at the company or to impart important information about the business. Making sure that all the participants are aware of their expected decorum at these meetings, and that they come prepared, will ensure successful meetings.

The keys to a successful business meeting:

- **Be prepared.**
  It is unprofessional to attend a meeting without adequate preparation—especially if you are expected to make a presentation. If possible, always try to obtain an agenda ahead of the meeting. If you are hosting the meeting, send the participants an agenda in advance,

- **Dress appropriately and be well groomed.**
  If the meeting is with older, more traditional clients, a jacket or suit and tie would be considered appropriate. Even if it is an in-house meeting, you might nevertheless pay particular attention to your attire, since it will be noticed.

- **Arrive on time or a few minutes early to make small talk with the participants.**
  Research shows that meetings that begin with small talk—especially with new clients—result in more successful meetings.

- **Introduce yourself.**
  As soon as you approach people you don't know or are approached by them, give your name and title. Always stand for an introduction so that you are able to engage a person on an equal, eye-to-eye level; and extend your hand as you give your greeting. The person who puts a hand out first comes across as confident and at ease.

- **Pay attention to names when you meet people so you can address them by name in the meeting.**
  If you concentrate and repeat the name as soon as you hear it, you stand a better chance of remembering it later. Use first names of individuals whom you have just met *only* after they give you permission. One thing that will help to keep everyone straight is to place their business cards in front of you in the order they are seated at the table.

- **Always switch off your cell phone—particularly if you are a junior member of the staff.**

- **If there is an established seating pattern, accept it.**
  If you are unsure of where to sit, wait for the senior members to sit down first before you take a seat.

- **Wait to be invited to take a seat.**
  If you have an appointment for an interview or a meeting with a new client at their office, don't sit down until your host invites you to do so and provides direction where to sit.

- **Let senior executives lead the discussions.**
  When discussions are under way, it's good business etiquette to allow more senior figures to contribute first and lead the way.

- **Never interrupt anyone, even if you strongly disagree.**
  Or, if it's necessary for the integrity of the meeting, be sure to interrupt as politely as you can and without raising your voice.

- **When you need to add something, be brief and ensure what you say is relevant.**
  At less formal, in-house meetings, give everyone a chance to contribute. According to a Google research study, when everyone gets a chance to talk, the team does well. If only one person or a small group speaks all of the time, they found the collective intelligence declines.

- **Show respect for the chair and the meeting's attendees.**
  Always address the chair unless it is clear that others are not doing so; and show respect for the chair and other attendees by not engaging in crosstalk

- **Do not allow challenges to your authority to go unanswered.**
  Be assertive; take charge. Don't let others rob you of your command of a room or a meeting. Parrying with humor is your best defense, but sometimes you need to reassert your authority more powerfully.

- **Matters discussed in the meeting should be considered confidential.**
  It's a serious breach of business etiquette to divulge information

to others about a meeting. Anything that's been discussed should be considered confidential.

- **Provide a next-steps summary at the end of the meeting.**
  Everyone should know what they will be expected to do following the meeting.

- **Follow up.**
  If you have been assigned a task to complete, be sure to complete it on time.

23

[SUCCESS]

Virtual Business Meeting Protocol

WITH THE NEW HYBRID WORKPLACE and ease of holding business meetings and conferences virtually with participants anywhere in the world, more and more virtual meetings and video conferences are being scheduled than ever before. If you keep uppermost in your mind that it is just like being there and comport yourself accordingly, you will make a positive impression.

It is just like being there in person.

The key to a successful video or telephone conference is to remember that you are in a meeting. Give your full attention to the participants just as you would if you were in the same room. In fact, the same guidelines for in-person formal meetings should be followed for virtual meetings. However, there are additional guidelines that are unique to virtual meetings.

Always assume that when you walk into the room, the microphones are already live to other locations! This helps prevent any extraneous pre-meeting conversations from being broadcast when you may not want to be heard by others.

The video-conferencing protocol checklist:

- **Follow standard in-person formal meeting protocol if hosting and/or attending a formal business meeting.**
  It is outlined on the previous page.

- **Polish your appearance and your environment.**
  Polish your appearance before taking the call—just as you would if you were attending an in-person meeting—and polish the environment surrounding you if it will be seen by the attendees. A tasteful, business-like virtual background is recommended.

  Prior to the call, use the picture-in-picture "near side" view function to see how you will appear to those on the other end of the call. Ensure you are visible within the frame, that your environment is adequately lit, and that there are no distractions in the background. Also make sure your line of sight is relatively level, and that you're not looking at your participants on the other side from an angle tilted too severely high or low.

- **Arrive early for the meeting.**
  Arriving early will allow time for testing the technical components like the angle of your laptop, camera, volume, lighting, and incoming view window to ensure you will be fully prepared for the meeting when it starts. Appearing calm and fully prepared when the meeting begins will make a positive impression and present you as a professional.

- **Check your volume before the meeting begins.**
  Make sure your volume is set at the right level for you to be clearly heard. You don't want to sound like you're shouting or can't be heard.

- **Eliminate any stray noises in the room or background.**
  Turn off alarms, put your landlines and cell phone on mute, and

if you have a dog or children, have them stay in another room until your conference is finished.

- **Check your camera and make any adjustments before the meeting or conference begins.**
  Once the meeting or video conference begins, make as few alterations to your camera angle or laptop as possible. Some modifications may be necessary, but keep in mind they can be distracting to the participants and person speaking.

- **Be courteous to other participants and expect others attending the conference to be courteous as well.**
  This means not talking when another person is speaking, not interrupting or speaking out of turn, and acknowledging or greeting other participants when they join the meeting.

- **Don't make distracting sounds.**
  As with any face-to-face meeting, side conversations can be distracting and are, in fact, rude and should be avoided. If you are eating, the sound will also be heard as well as seen. Wait to have a snack or lunch until the meeting is over—unless it's a lunch meeting, in which case eating would be acceptable.

- **Speak clearly and slowly and make sure you pause for a few seconds after asking a question.**

- **Keep body movements minimal; move slowly and naturally.**
  It is especially important that you avoid fidgeting since it signals you are bored with the meeting or may have had too much coffee. Movements are magnified when only the upper portion of your body, or simply your head, is seen on the screen.

- **Maintain eye contact.**
  Focus on looking into the camera on your laptop. You may need

to place your laptop on a stack of books to line up the camera with your eyes.

- **If you are a participant, bring attention to yourself by stating your name before addressing the group—especially if it's a large group.**

- **Yield the floor to remote team members first.**
  The host of the meeting should introduce the remote team to the in-house team members.

- **Avoid the temptation to multi-task during the meeting.**
  Be fully present at the meeting. Constantly looking at your computer display, talking on your cell phone or to someone in the room with you, typing on your keyboard, checking your texts or emails, or Web surfing shows a lack of professionalism and respect for the meeting and those attending it. And don't eat or drink anything if you are hosting the meeting or are going to be speaking. Video conferences are much more interpersonal and interactive than telephone calls or emails, and attentiveness and nonverbal cues matter.

- **If no one on your end of the call is talking, you can mute your microphone.**
  The video conference system won't distinguish between relevant and irrelevant sounds and will hone in on sidebar gossip just as readily as the core meeting points. When you or someone on your team wants to speak, simply click the "unmute" button and make your point. Then, when you've had your say, return to the mute mode.

- **Upgrade your equipment.**
  If you want to appear and sound your best, consider purchasing a good quality stereo microphone with noise cancellation and a

standalone webcam for virtual meetings, presentations, and interviews. In most cases, your laptop's built-in camera and microphone are not the best quality and can prevent you from coming across as polished and professional as possible.

- **Be considerate of time zones, making sure the meeting is held at a convenient time for all, if possible.**

24

[SUCCESS]

Be the Quintessential Professional at the Office

THE SAME THOUGHTFULNESS YOU EXTEND to your family and friends should be extended to those with whom you come into contact at the office. The essence of etiquette is courtesy, and the greatest courtesy you can exhibit at the office is to ensure that all your actions take into consideration the comfort and enjoyment of everyone around you; and to conduct yourself in a manner that makes the office a pleasant, productive place to work. When you show your coworkers, clients, and customers your best self, you set yourself apart from the competition and create long-lasting professional relationships.

Guidelines for proper business office decorum:

- **Be on time.**
  If you're late on a regular basis, people will notice. While everyone has the occasional late morning, it's not fair to your coworkers to feel the rules don't apply to you. The same holds true for business meetings. It is never a good idea to arrive late for a business meeting. And never intentionally keep a client, or anyone else, waiting.

- **Extend a friendly greeting.**
  When greeting a new client or existing client at the office, it's good form to address them by their name, make eye contact, give them a firm handshake, and make them feel welcome. If you already know the person, but others in your office don't, it's necessary to make the proper introductions.

- **Maintain appropriate conduct.**
  If you are in a conservative business environment, your body language should be controlled and formal. There should be no laughter in the hallways, no walking around whistling and humming a tune, and no spontaneous outbursts of emotions or feelings. If you're in a casual business environment, your body language can be less controlled and more informal. It's okay to laugh a bit and socialize a bit to build rapport when a more personal expression is acceptable as part of fulfilling business expectations. It doesn't mean, however, that you can slack off or behave in a silly or immature manner.

- **Keep your desk neat.**
  Your desk or cubicle should be an extension of yourself. If it's messy and cluttered, you'll probably have difficulty locating necessary items. In addition, business associates will not regard you in a favorable light due to the untidiness of your workspace. No one likes to wait—particularly clients or senior management—while you attempt to unearth a missing item from under a mound of papers.

- **Pay attention.**
  Whether in a meeting, on the phone, or sitting in a coworker's office, stay alert and pay attention. It's bad form to be caught with your mind wandering, or checking your messages on your cell phone or PDA, and to have no clue as to what actually took place. Be a good listener and take notes. Don't interrupt unless you absolutely have to.

- **Avoid having lengthy personal conversations on the phone when others can hear you.**
  No one wants to listen to you arguing with your husband or wife or telling your doctor about a health issue in great detail.

- **Steer clear of personal habits that annoy.**
  Even the smallest personal habit can appear magnified in a closed office setting. Things like constantly clearing your throat, blowing your nose, combing your hair every five minutes, doing your nails or putting on makeup at your desk, even taking vitamins—can be annoying and distracting to others and make a bad impression. Use the restroom for doing things that are best done in private.

- **Ask before borrowing a coworker's office supplies.**
  Extend the same courtesy to others that you would expect from them. It is never a good idea to simply borrow whatever you'd like from another person's desk without asking them first if it's okay.

- **Knock before entering a closed office or walking uninvited into a teammate's cubicle.**
  Always knock on a closed door, then wait until the person inside tells you to come in. Although a cubicle may not have a door, do not assume it means you can walk into it without being invited. If you've just stopped by to chat, ask if it's a good time. If someone stops by to chat with you when you're in the midst of a project and don't wish to be interrupted, be polite and let them know it isn't a good time.

- **Make small talk, but avoid becoming overly involved in coworkers' personal lives.**
  It's natural to be interested in your coworkers' lives and want to be friends with some of them, but you should avoid becoming

too involved. Be brief and discreet if you discuss personal issues at the office; remember, you're there to be productive—not spend an inordinate amount of time socializing. However, spending some time exchanging pleasantries with your coworkers is advised since it will help build the rapport necessary for successfully working together.

- **Avoid behavior that could be misconstrued.**
  At one time, a little harmless flirting or complimentary remarks about someone's appearance might have been considered acceptable. No longer. Now that there's a heightened awareness of discrimination and harassment in the workplace, flirtatious comments and personal compliments may not be welcome by the recipient and could lead to your dismissal from the company.

- **Watch what you eat at your desk.**
  Anything that's going to offend others, such as food that has a strong odor, should be avoided at the office. If you're in an area where others will see you eat, mind your manners. When you're finished, throw away any leftover food and disposable containers in the appropriate waste can. Nothing should be left on your desk; and you shouldn't even eat at your desk if you sit in a public area where clients walk by.

- **Follow the rules established for the office kitchen.**
  Unless the office refrigerator is stocked with complimentary food, do not assume anything you see in it is yours for the taking. If you didn't put the food in it, it is not yours to eat. Be sure to take your leftovers home or throw them out before they're past their expiration date. And if you use the last cup of coffee in the coffee maker, tell the person whose job it is to make more. Clean up after yourself before you leave the kitchen.

- **Be mindful of what you heat in the microwave or oven.**
  Fish, for instance, is absolutely unacceptable. Anything that has a strong odor that can permeate the office should be avoided.

- **Courtesy, consideration, and a respect for others are prime requisites for an office to function as a comfortable, safe and pleasant place to work.**

25

SUCCESS

Polished, Professional Business Communications

IN THE 24/7 WORLD OF business today, we use all forms of communication to connect with coworkers, clients, and others to accomplish our tasks. It is extremely important both for your image and that of the company you represent that all communications be polished and professional. Any written communication should be thoroughly proofread to ensure correct grammar, spelling, punctuation, facts, and names.

Telephone Etiquette

- When making a phone call, begin by identifying yourself and your company. If you are returning someone's call, include that information as well.
  "Good morning/afternoon. This is Daniel Simpson from Goldman Sachs. May I speak to Mr. Clinton in your marketing department." Or, if you are returning a call, after identifying yourself, you would say, "I am returning Mr. Clinton's call. Is he available to speak with me"?
- Always try to return a phone call the same day or within 24 hours. It demonstrates you value the caller and consider the call important enough to return it without delay. Phone calls that are returned quickly can make the difference between winning or

losing an important account, or being chosen or passed up for a career opportunity.
- When returning someone's phone call, consider their time zone so you don't call before or after normal business hours. With so many people working from home these days, a phone call could awaken their family at an inconvenient time. It's best not to call before 9:00 a.m. for a business or personal call, or after 6:00 p.m. unless you've made an appointment to talk after that time.
- If you have call waiting, refrain from answering another call when talking to your boss, customer, or client. If you're expecting an important call, let clients and coworkers know ahead of time before putting them on hold. Avoid putting someone on hold more than once.

Voicemail: Greeting

Record a pleasant-sounding, clearly-spoken professional message on your voicemail, such as *"Hello, you have reached Bill Thornton at the New York Times. Please leave your name, telephone number, and a brief message and a convenient time to return your call. Thank you."*

Voicemail: Leaving a Message

Speak slowly and clearly when leaving a voicemail message. Identify yourself, your company, your telephone number, the purpose of your call, the date and time, and a convenient time to return your call. Repeat your telephone number at the end of your message.

Text Messaging

Text messaging for business is now acceptable, and the use of it has increased dramatically in the last few years due to its speed of communication. It's especially useful when there's a sense of urgency. Texts should be short, but do your best to avoid acronyms and abbreviations, using grammatical sentences and completely spelled words instead. Texts should not replace detailed emails or phone conversations. When you receive a text message, respond promptly unless you are unavailable.

Speakerphone

Always ask permission before putting someone on speakerphone, and let them know the names of any other people in the room with you. For conference calls, you should formally introduce everyone at the beginning of the call.

Email Etiquette

Use the subject line to inform. An email's importance is often determined by the subject line. An email without a subject is likely to get deleted. Keep the subject line brief, specific, and relevant. For a short email, you can use the subject line only: "Confirming lunch today at 12:00 p.m. See you soon."

- Treat emails like business letters. It's better to be too formal than too casual when you want to make a good impression.
- List recipients alphabetically or according to hierarchy when there is more than one. This also applies to the 'cc' line.
- Keep emails brief, but not abrupt. Brevity is key when sending email, but you do not want to come across as rude.
- Be mindful when using the 'Reply All' function. If you receive an email that was sent to a multitude of other people, reply only to those who require a response.
- Respond to emails quickly. If someone emails you with a question and you don't have an immediate answer or the time to fully answer it, a simple acknowledgment with a promise that you'll give the question your full attention at a given point is preferable to not answering at all.
- Tell others when you are not available. Use the 'Out-of-Office' auto-respond feature if you plan to be out of the office for an extended period of time.
- Do not shout. Using all UPPERCASE LETTERS is considered cyber shouting and rude.
- Avoid emailing confidential information; use the telephone or meet in person. Emails can be duplicated, forwarded, and

printed, so don't send or say anything you wouldn't want repeated or posted in your company newsletter.
- Do not use fancy decorations, vivid colors, flashing symbols, or bouncing smiley faces (emoticons) for business communications. Also avoid sarcasm or subtle humor unless you know the recipient will get it. If in doubt, err toward the formal and polite, particularly if you are not well acquainted with the recipient or you are dealing with foreign clients who may not understand our sarcasm or humor.
- Avoid mood mail. Email messages that convey strong emotions can easily be misinterpreted and should not be used in potentially volatile circumstances, such as firing or reprimanding someone or ending a contract. Never send an email when you're angry. Take time to cool down, then reread the email before sending it to make sure it doesn't contain anything you will regret later.
- Do not use email to reply to correspondence or an invitation that was not sent by email or does not supply an email address.

Business Letters

Although email is the most-used format for written communications in business today, there will be times when a business letter should be sent instead. A business letter is a formal document that has a set formula. It includes contact information at the top of the letter, a salutation, such as Dear Mr. Worthington or Ms. Flanagan, the body of the letter, an appropriate close, such as regards or sincerely, and a signature.

In general, it's best to keep the letter brief and limited to one page. The first paragraph should explain the purpose of the letter, with the next two or three paragraphs providing the specifics. Use the closing paragraph to summarize your reason for writing. Lastly, thank the recipient for their consideration and mention possible next steps or plans for meeting.

When sending a business letter, use the office stationery with your company's letterhead and, possibly, your name. Every executive should have fine quality business stationery with matching envelopes, even if it's rarely used.

Thank You Notes

There are many reasons and occasions for writing a thank you note for business, including: after meeting with an important client; after an interview with a prospective client; when you've been interviewed for a job; when you receive a gift; when you've been given tickets to a sporting or cultural event; and when you've been treated to a business meal. Saying thank you enhances your profile. Not only will people remember you took the time to write a thank you note, they will also consider you a thoughtful, appreciative person—good traits for a business person to possess.

Every business executive should have a supply of fine quality correspondence cards with their name or company engraved on them, along with matching envelopes. A hand-written thank you note is always better than one that is typed; but if your handwriting is less than ideal, typing your note is acceptable. Three or four sentences will suffice.

Addressing and Double-Checking Envelopes

Always make sure you've spelled a person's name correctly. Address the envelope with the person's title—Mr., Ms., etc.—and full name, followed with their business title and, of course, their full address. Your return address should be printed or engraved on the front, upper left corner of the envelope.

26

SUCCESS

Social Media and Networking Guidelines to Follow

SOME COMPANIES ENCOURAGE THEIR EMPLOYEES to make use of social networking tools like blogs, Facebook, Instagram, and Twitter; and most now have at least one full-time person devoted to promoting their company on social media. Done intelligently and with specific guidelines, social networking can help build brand recognition, improve the flow of information between companies and their consumers, and increase customer loyalty and engagement.

> *If you make customers unhappy in the physical world, they might each tell 6 friends. If you make customers unhappy on the Internet, they can each tell 6,000 friends.*
> —Jeff Bezos

Many companies discourage or outright forbid their employees from engaging in online socializing about the company and its employees. They realize that such activities can result in a huge leak of sensitive, confidential, and often misleading information. Therefore, one of the first things you should do when you join a new company is find out what the company's policy is regarding social networking. It is imperative to comply with your company policy or you risk disciplinary action, termination, or even a lawsuit.

Be mindful of the fact that there is a difference between social networking for work and social networking at work. The company policy may allow you to participate, but not during normal working hours—unless, of course, corporate communications is part of your job description.

Social media guidelines for your professional life:

- **Communicate a consistent, positive presence.**
  Whether you use social media for personal or professional purposes, it is often the first impression others have of you; and once formed, it's difficult to change. So, communicate a consistent presence that reflects well upon you.

- **Treat each social media page differently.**
  Always be professional, but especially so on LinkedIn. On Facebook, you can use a lighter tone and let people see a glimpse of your personal life, although you will still need to maintain your spotless reputation.

- **Write down a social media goal and only post things that reflect that goal and your values. Post just once a day on most sites.**
  More frequent posts are okay on Twitter.

- **Ask for permission.**
  Before posting anything that shows or tags another person in your personal or professional life, or shares personal information about a coworker, ask for permission to do so.

- **If someone is rude or profane on your page, delete the post immediately.**
  You are known by those with whom you associate. When others engage in name calling or post inflammatory remarks on your feed, it reflects badly on you.

- **Be sure the information you post is accurate.**
  If you are stating something as fact, make sure it is fact, not opinion or wishful thinking. Citing references or sources makes what you post more credible.

- **Clearly state that your opinion and viewpoints are yours, and do not represent the position of your employers.**
  Keep in mind, however, that trying to keep a separation between the two often doesn't work, as anything you say is quite often a reflection of your company or can be seen to be the viewpoint of your company since you work there.

- **Engage in intelligent dialogue with others.**
  Find out who else is blogging about the topics that interest you. Comment on their posts and link to their blogs. You'll help build your network of resources and online credibility.

- **Keep personal conversations, arguments, and political views off social networking sites.**
  And don't discuss sensitive personal issues on Facebook—especially if you've friended coworkers.

- **Consider potential conflict of interest repercussions.**
  If you "friend-request" a contact that will put either of you in an awkward or comprising position, perhaps you should think twice before friending that person. You should also think twice about being friends with your boss on sites such as Facebook unless everything you post is meant for a general audience.

- **Watch your spelling and grammar.**
  Whether it is a positive first or continued positive impression you want to make, attention to detail will be noticed. Incorrect spelling and poor grammar will reflect negatively on you.

- **Review what you're saying before clicking "submit."**
  Doing so is not only a reflection on you, but on your company as well, even if you do publish a disclaimer.

- **What you post may last forever.**
  Think carefully before you post anything on the internet. It's virtually impossible to remove anything once it has been posted

- **Don't share company secrets.**
  If something isn't published in a press release or an official company website, don't reveal anything about your company.

27

SUCCESS

Outshine the Competition to Land a Job

More than anything else, I hire for attitude. Skills can be learned. I'll take attitude any day over a good skill set.

—G.J. Hart, CEO

BUSINESS EXECUTIVES TODAY FACE MORE challenges than any have experienced in the past. Therefore, it is not enough now to have the technical skills and education required to qualify for a job or to successfully perform it once hired. The most sought-after job skills employers seek now are soft or "people" skills, along with communication skills and flexibility. Possessing these skills will enable you to distinguish yourself from the competition, land a job, and help you develop and maintain business in today's fast-paced, challenging, and complex business environment.

The following plan will help you present yourself and your qualifications in the best manner possible to ensure that you have the advantage over your competition in your mission to land a job–whether you're unemployed, working and would like to change jobs, or an entrepreneur meeting with potential investors to raise funding for a new project.

A Plan of Action for Outshining the Competition

- **Begin with a positive attitude.**
  Everything you do is informed by your attitude. According to Nicolas Boothman, author of *Attitude Is Everything,* "The quality of your attitude controls the quality and appearance of everything you do." Your attitude and professional image help form the first impression others have of you.

  Very few people find searching for a job or going for an interview a pleasant experience; but, if you go for an interview with the same attitude that you have when you go to the dentist, it's unlikely you will present yourself in a positive manner. Your attitude is reflected in your facial expressions, body language, and voice. It's very difficult to cover up a negative attitude. If you don't feel good about yourself and your qualifications, it would be better to wait until you do; otherwise, you will be wasting your time.

  Whether it requires getting into shape, buying a new suit, seeking therapy, or going back to school to update your job skills, I would recommend that you consider these options before beginning your job search. When you go for an interview, projecting a positive, winning attitude and confidence in yourself will be relayed to the person interviewing you and make them more likely to view you in the same manner. People like people with positive, cheerful personalities, not people who project a defensive, "woe is me" attitude.

  In a recent survey of college admissions officers, one admissions officer of an Ivy League university said, "Some 70 percent of kids who apply are qualified to come to school here; and we have space for one in ten. We can be as choosy as we like. It almost always comes down to whether or not you're a likeable person. Let's face it, some people are just more affable and more likeable than others." The same can be said of the job market: there are many more qualified people than there are positions for them. The jobs will go to the people with the best attitudes and ability to relate to others.

People like people with positive, cheerful personalities.

- **Create a power presence.**
  Appearances matter tremendously in first impressions. With this in mind, it would not make sense to consider going for an interview until you've done a thorough review of your appearance and the impact you make on others. Your appearance includes not only your physical being, but also your attire, your grooming, and your deportment. The more "put together" your appearance, the more you leave a positive impression. If you have recently left your job after being with the same company for many years, you may not have had to worry about your appearance, but now you do.

  When you interview for a job, people consider your entire package. Research has shown that the number one reason companies reject an applicant after the first interview is poor personal appearance. "People buy you with their eyes. The visual overwhelms the verbal," writes Harry Beckwith, author of *You, Inc.* Make sure that your personal package is as polished as your resume. Know the company's dress code policy before interviewing. In general, it's better to dress conservatively and err on the formal side rather than be underdressed. The same advice applies if your interview will be online; dress and grooming will be as closely evaluated as if you were meeting in person. As for your shoes, even if your interviewer can't see them, wearing the right ones will make you feel more put together and professional.

People buy you with their eyes.

- **Hone your soft skills.**
  In the competitive job market, it isn't enough to be able to do your job well. Success in getting, keeping, and advancing in a job

depends 85 percent on soft, or people, skills, and 15 percent on technical knowledge and skills, according to three separate research projects by Harvard University, the Carnegie Foundation, and the Stanford Research Institute. Knowing the rules of business etiquette and protocol and knowing how to handle yourself in social situations are key elements in being successful. If you have more than one interview with a company, it is likely that one will be a luncheon meeting. Nothing is more telling about a person than his table manners. Are you ready for a luncheon interview?

The jobs will go to the best and the brightest and the most socially skillful!

- **Critique your assets and qualifications.**
  Your greatest asset is self-knowledge. Know what your special abilities are, what you like to do, what your true interests and passions are, what you do best, and, of course, what you are qualified to do based upon your education and experience. Be prepared to discuss the value you will provide to the company, along with specific examples of what you have accomplished in the past, relating them to what you can achieve in the future. Be creative and flexible in your approach to job hunting. Look at the transferable skills you have which can be used in a variety of industries.

Before you can sell your qualifications, you have to sell yourself!

- **Give your resume an edge.** Modern resumes are different: they are more succinct and results-oriented. Employers today buy results and are less interested in reading a laundry list of skills. Think about the jobs you've had and how you either made money or saved money for the companies you worked for.

Another difference now is that savvy job seekers are beginning their resumes with personal brand statements. A personal brand statement, according to Tom Peters, "is a statement that identifies the qualities or characteristics that make you distinctive from your competitors–what you do that adds remarkable, measurable, distinguished, or distinctive value." It should not be more than two sentences.

Whatever you can tastefully do to make your resume stand out from the competition is also recommended. Recruiters are getting so many resumes now that even small efforts like using the corporate logos to represent your previous employers can help make yours get noticed. Or consider turning your resume into a marketing package. After all, you are marketing a product: You!

Never send a resume without a cover letter, whether by email or regular mail. The cover letter shouldn't exceed one page, and it should convey why you're seeking a job with that particular company. If you are emailing your resume, follow it with a hard copy sent by mail. Remember, targeted job searches are generally much more successful than mass mailings.

You are marketing a product: You!

- **Prepare diligently for your interview.**
If you are fortunate enough to be granted an interview, prepare for it: rehearse, rehearse, rehearse! Whether it's with your career coach, your wife, a tape recorder, or in front of your dog, make sure you have your lines straight. You should have a short and well-thought-out reason why you're looking for a job, as well as why you are interested in working for the company you're interviewing with. You don't have to apologize or make excuses for why you don't currently have a job, or why you're looking for one. Be positive! Being granted an interview is the same as being invited to a party: you were invited because someone wanted

you to be there. And keep in mind that, according to Career Builder®, it takes an average of seventeen interviews to get one offer.

It's also a good thing to keep in mind that in today's business environment, companies are looking for people who are flexible, have a can-do attitude, and have a passion for what they're doing. They want team players who will work together to help their company succeed during these difficult times. At some point during the interview, it would be advisable to let your interviewer know that you are this kind of person: adaptable and willing to do whatever you can to help the company succeed.

- **Shine at networking events.**
According to Phyllis Korkki, a writer for the *New York Times*, "You are more likely to find a job through someone you know. The larger the circle of people, and the more you cultivate it, the better off you will be." Everyone learns the technical skills required for their jobs, but not everyone places importance on learning how to graciously interact with others in social situations. Learning how to shine at networking events with your power, presence, and style is one of the most important things you can learn when looking for a job.

You are more likely to find a job through someone you know.

Interview etiquette tips that will land you the job:

- **Dress for success.**
The way you represent yourself at an interview is an indication of how you will represent the company if hired. Your attire should fit with the company culture. In other words, look like you already work there and signal that you are a person who is going places.

- **Be on time.**
  When you're late, it is not only rude, it also sends a message that you don't really care about the interview. In fact, it is advisable to be ten minutes early to compose yourself before the meeting.

- **Be polite to the receptionist.**
  The receptionist is the gate keeper; if you're rude to her, it sends the message that you will be rude to other people in the company. People skills are considered to be as, if not more, important than your ability to do a job.

- **Never underestimate your handshake.**
  Stand up when you meet someone, introduce yourself, make eye contact, and offer a firm handshake. Did you know that your abilities may be judged by a three-second handshake? Your handshake speaks loudly about your professionalism, credibility, and confidence. It communicates a powerful nonverbal message before you speak. A firm handshake conveys "I'm interested in you and confident in my business skills," whereas a weak handshake may be interpreted as "I'm unsure of myself and I'm uncomfortable being here and meeting you."

- **Walk into the room with authority and poise.**
  Keep your shoulders back, spine erect. and movements smooth when walking into your interviewer's office. This conveys confidence in yourself.

- **Do not take a seat until offered one.**
  If you do, you will appear to be disrespectful and presumptuous. Once you do take a seat, sit erect. Slouching shows a lack of professionalism and is a reflection on your personality.

- **Actively participate in the interview.**
  Make eye contact, lean forward to show interest, nod your head,

and smile when appropriate. Participating actively in an interview helps you establish a rapport with your interviewer. Try to find common ground. People like to hire people with whom they are comfortable and with whom they have a good rapport. And finally, be upbeat and personable without being overly familiar.

- **Be prepared with your script.**
This includes your 15-second personal introduction "pitch" that directly correlates with your personal brand statement. You'll also want to mention your situation (why you're looking for a new opportunity), your job experience, qualifications, and why you think you would be a good fit for the company. When you're asked to talk about yourself, this is your opportunity to present yourself in the best possible light. Make sure you make the most of it without seeming overly confident and arrogant. And, very importantly, don't act like you assume you have the job before it is offered to you.

- **Ask questions.**
Always have questions ready when an interviewer asks if you have any. Not doing so implies you're not interested in the company. If you have thoroughly prepared for the interview, you will have taken a list of questions with you.

- **Thank the Interviewer.**
Always thank the interviewer when you leave an interview and follow up with a thank-you note. According to Harry Beckwith, "three in four executives consider applicants' thank-you notes in making hiring decisions." Apparently, however, only one in three applicants sends a thank-you note. A thank-you note only needs to be four sentences, and should simply thank the person for the interview; it should not be a pretense for making another pitch.

28

| SUCCESS |

What New College Graduates Need to Know and Do to Launch Successful Careers

The greater danger for most of us lies not in setting our aim too high and falling short; but in setting our aim too low, and achieving our mark.
—Michelangelo

The top 10 tips for new college graduates:

1. **Know the proper protocol for introducing yourself and others.**
   Always have a pre-planned self-introduction for every interview and networking event you attend—one that will stimulate interest in you.

2. **Shake hands with a firm grip, direct eye contact, and erect posture.**
   Confident body language speaks volumes about your credibility as a person who is going places.

3. **Suit up for success.**
   Wear appropriate business attire and always make sure you are

well-groomed when you go on a job interview or to a business meeting. Polished shoes translate to attention to detail. A polished appearance opens doors!

4. **Cultivate a strong, clear speaking voice.**
   Enunciate your words and do not use slang, foul language, or filler words. Knowing how to communicate clearly and effectively is essential to your success.

5. **Polish your electronic and written communications.**
   Be professional: conduct yourself in a business-like manner at all times, using appropriate business language. Use correct spelling, grammar and punctuation.

6. **Be professional when using your phone for business.**
   Always identify yourself when placing and answering a call. Be prepared to leave a voicemail when you place a call, since over half of all calls placed go to voicemail.

7. **Know what is appropriate and what does not reflect positively on you when using your social networking tools.**
   Every communication in both the virtual and real world is an opportunity to make a good impression.

8. **Master the art of mingling, networking, and making small talk.**
   Being skillful at mingling, networking, and small talk will not only help you get a job, it will also help you stand out in your new job.

9. **Perfect your dining skills and table manners.**
   You may be invited to have lunch with a potential employer so that he or she can observe your table manners. Demonstrating fine dining skills and stellar table manners greatly enhance your odds of landing a job.

10. Demonstrate good manners at all times!
   Civility counts! People remember and are impressed with people who have good manners.

PART THREE

Your Etiquette Guide to the Social World

29

SUCCESS

Be a Courteous Man About Town

Fine manners need the support of fine manners in others.
—Ralph Waldo Emerson

Top 25 dos:

1. Do keep to the right when walking on a sidewalk, except when passing; and try to walk at the same pace as the other pedestrians.
2. Do let others exit elevators, buildings, and public transportation before you attempt to enter them.
3. Do hold doors open for individuals following closely behind you or for someone who may need a little help entering a building, an elevator, or public transportation. A host should always pull the door open for visitors and motion for them to walk ahead.
4. Do lead the way by going through a door first when you're a host escorting a visitor into a building unfamiliar to him or her. Push the door, pass through, and then hold it open.
5. Do yield to older people, those with disabilities, slow walkers, and those carrying packages when going through a revolving door.
6. Do go through the revolving door first if it is not moving when you are with a date. If it is already in motion, allow your date to go through first. As a host escorting a client, you should go through first, saying to your guest that you will go first and wait for them on the other side.

7. Do move to the back of the elevator when you get on to allow room for others to enter; and if you find yourself next to the floor-control panel, it's considered good manners to ask "Which floor?" to others entering the elevator, and then push the button. If there are ladies waiting to enter the elevator, allow them to get on first. "Ladies first" still matters.
8. Do move to the right side after stepping onto an escalator to allow others to pass you if they wish. Leave a step between you and the person in front of you if you can; and, unless you're with a small child, you should not stand next to someone; nor should you put a shopping bag down beside you. Lastly, once you arrive at a floor, exit quickly to allow riders behind you to get off.
9. Do be mindful of others if you are talking or texting on your cell phone when walking down the street, getting on public transportation, or walking up or down stairs. Especially try to avoid talking on your phone in a store when paying a cashier for an item.
10. Do have your token, fare card, cash, or ticket out and ready before getting in line to enter a bus or subway so that you don't keep those behind you waiting.
11. Do give up your seat to someone who may need it more than you—the elderly, a caregiver with small children, a pregnant woman—when you're taking public transportation.
12. Do keep your body language controlled and confined to the space within your seat. Don't put your bags on the seat next to you –particularly if there are not enough seats for everyone.
13. Do use earphones when listening to music in public places or when you're taking public transportation; and be sure your music is not so loud it can be heard by a person sitting next to you. If you accidentally cross someone's personal space, take your earphones out and graciously apologize.
14. Do be generous and let the other person take a taxi if the two of you hail one at the same time. Do not run to a taxi that someone else has already hailed and take it.

15. Do be mindful of others when you are talking or texting on your cell phone in public places: Save your private conversations for private locations.
16. Do be sensitive to others' enjoyment at restaurants, movies, or any other performance or cultural event by moderating your use of cameras and videos, keeping your voice low during conversation, not talking on your cell phone, and by conducting yourself with decorum.
17. Do be ready to place your order as soon as you get in line at a Starbucks or any coffee shop to avoid keeping the barista and others behind you waiting. Absolutely don't ask everyone to wait for you to place your order until you have finished a phone call.
18. Do offer a greeting to the salespeople when entering boutiques or small stores, and say thank you when you leave. And do leave stacks of clothes as you found them—not in a disheveled mess.
19. Do pick up after your dog when it does its business, which should not be on the sidewalk or someone's private property.
20. Do eat in restaurants or other appropriate places such as a park, or where tables and chairs have been set up for this purpose—not on public transportation or walking down the street.
21. Do show respect for city streets, public places, public transportation, and taxis. Throw your trash in trash cans instead of littering.
22. Do cross the street at crosswalks and wait until you see the walk sign flash when crossing busy city streets.
23. Do be sure to allow pedestrians, bikers and runners the right of way when driving through the city. Obey traffic signs and signals and use your turn signal when you intend to make a turn.
24. Do obey the rules of the road when biking through the city, and always give pedestrians the right of way—even if they're not following the established safety rules for crossing the street.
25. Do be polite and use the magic words we all appreciate hearing. Say "Please" and "Thank you" to the waitstaff in restaurants, salespeople in stores, and whenever or wherever appropriate.

30

[SUCCESS]

A Modern Manners Checklist for Young Men

ETIQUETTE EVOLVES TO ADAPT TO the times, but manners are a constant because they are more about how we treat other people rather than strict rules for how things should be done. Manners are about being mindful of others and showing respect for them. Good manners never go out of style! Put your best manners on display when you want to communicate respect for and a sensitive awareness of others.

Gentle reminders for young men to keep in mind:

- **Put your mobile device away when you are with other people.**
  I'm sure you frequently hear this, "He never puts his cell phone away." If you would try to discipline yourself to put your mobile device away when you're with a date, your relatives, or anyone you respect, it would be noticed and appreciated.

- **Make polite conversation.**
  When you show interest in others and ask questions about them, they will find you likeable. They will also think you are well mannered. When you're invited to a social event or someone's home, you should always go prepared with a few conversation topics they would find interesting. In other words, plan on being sociable

and showing interest in the people you know or are meeting for the first time.

- **Make eye contact.**
  When you are speaking to another person, it's polite to make eye contact with them. It shows respect for the person, and it also shows that you're confident. Force yourself to look others in the eye when greeting, talking, and especially listening. Avoid staring, however, since that makes people feel uncomfortable.

- **Mind your posture.**
  Stand and sit erect. Slouching makes you look lazy, disinterested, and disrespectful of the person with whom you are speaking or eating. It doesn't take much effort, but will make a world of difference in how you are perceived, since erect posture gives the impression of confidence, poise, and respect.

- **Be gracious and appreciative.**
  Use the magic words you learned when you were a child. Any time you want something, say, "Please." And when someone does something for you, gives you a gift, or hosts you at their home for the weekend, be sure to thank them. What about writing a thank-you note? It would be very classy if you sent a hand-written note, but an email or even a text would make you seem more appreciative than not sending any note. Lastly, when someone says, "Thank you" to you for something you have done for them, say, "You're welcome" or "It was my pleasure." Saying, "No problem" always implies that somehow it might have been.

- **Dress for your audience.**
  Acceptable modern dressing is certainly more casual today, but there are times when a t-shirt or hoodie and sneakers aren't appropriate. Even when Mark Zuckerberg testified in front of Congress last year, he wore a suit and tie because that is the

standard in that arena. So, if you are a man, I would recommend you have at least one blazer—black or navy blue—and one suit, with a pair of dress shoes. You never know when you will need them.

- **Be well groomed.**
This should go without saying, but I will tell you that, regardless of your attire, your grooming should be polished. Look in the mirror before you go out. If you're wearing a shirt that should be ironed and tucked in, then by all means press it and tuck it in. If you're wearing leather shoes, they should be polished.

- **Polish your table manners.**
You never know when good table manners will come in handy—like when you're having dinner with your significant other or their parents, or when your second interview with a company is over lunch. Brushing up on your table manners can only be a good thing. You may never attend a formal six-course meal at Buckingham Palace, but you will be attending many dinners where you'll be judged by your conduct at the table.

- **Refrain from constantly photographing yourself and everything you see and do for Instagram.**
Be selective about taking your phone out to take photographs—especially when you're with someone from the "older" generation. Even when you're out with friends your own age, it might be nice if you focused on them instead of being distracted. And you don't need to post everything you photograph on Instagram or Facebook.

- **Practice proper meeting and greeting skills.**
Nothing makes a better first or lasting impression than offering your hand for a firm handshake accompanied by a smile and appropriate greeting for a person you are meeting—whether

you've met before or are meeting for the first time. Be mindful of the fact that, when you're with friends, relatives, or business colleagues, it's your responsibility to introduce them if you encounter someone they don't know or who doesn't know them.

- **Offer to help with the cleanup.**
  If you are invited to someone's home for dinner, always offer to help with the dishes at the end of the meal. They may decline your offer, but will appreciate the fact that you made it. It shows you were brought up well.

- **Be considerate of your friends when dining out.**
  When eating out with a group of friends, pay attention to what everyone is ordering. It's a good idea to order the same number of courses, as well as drinks within the same price range. Ordering more courses, the most expensive entrée, and more glasses of wine than everyone else, and then saying "Let's just split it" at the end of the meal is very inconsiderate. If someone treats you to dinner, offer to pay the tip; or if it's a friend, tell them you will treat next time.

- **Keep your apartment neat for both expected and unexpected guests.**
  If you share an apartment with someone—or even if you don't—start developing the habit of straightening your apartment on a daily basis. Put clothes away, make your bed, put your dishes in the dishwasher, run the vacuum cleaner, etc. It not only shows respect for your roommate, it will make you feel more responsible and in charge of your life.

- **Always have cash on hand for gratuities.**
  Now that you are on your own, it's a good idea to have some cash on hand since you'll be the one to tip the delivery person when he brings your dinner, the doorman when he gets you a taxi, and

the maître d' at a restaurant when he gets you a special table. I know it's uncommon for young people to carry cash now, but most in the service industry prefer it. Just have an envelope full of ones and fives for when you need them—especially if you're traveling.

- **Don't point at people.**
  Sometimes it's hard to identify the person you're talking about using words alone. That said, however, pointing at people is still a social faux pas. Pointing makes people feel singled out and can make them assume you're gossiping about them, even if all you're actually doing is complimenting their outfit from afar.

- **Be kind and thoughtful when using social media.**
  Now that you're an adult, you must know words can be hurtful. They can be especially hurtful as well as exceedingly embarrassing if all the world can see what you've written about someone. Think also of your friends and family members when writing something inflammatory or controversial. Not only will it affect the way others view you, it will also have an impact on how they view people associated with you. Instead, consider having a private conversation rather than sharing your disagreement or heated exchange publicly.

31

| SUCCESS |

Be a Gentleman with a Lady

CHIVALRY IS NOT DEAD. LONG live chivalry! While a gentleman is no longer expected to throw his coat over a puddle so his female companion doesn't get her shoes wet, there are still some expectations women have of men. A man with beautiful manners is hard to resist. Of course, women also want him to be charming, have a sense of humor, be sensitive, and wear nice shoes!

Chivalry is not dead! Long live chivalry!

The courting game usually begins with a date. A man asks a woman out for dinner so they can get to know each other and see if they enjoy being together. Today, however, a woman may be the one extending the invitation, and that is perfectly acceptable. Today too, members of the same gender often date. Regardless of who extends the invitation, a date should be enjoyable; and each party should put his or her best foot forward to ensure that it is.

Courtly manners for a gentleman to keep in mind:

- **For a formal date, give her at least a few days' notice.**
  Should you call or text to ask her out? It all depends on your age and how you have been communicating. A telephone call is a

much warmer way to begin a relationship. Electronic communications can seem a little cold.

- **Make an effort to look your best.**
  Dress appropriately for the restaurant or event you'll be attending. Wear clothes that fit well, suit you, and are contemporary. Dressing poorly shows laziness and will do nothing to make you look good. Furthermore, it shows a lack of respect for your date who has more than likely made an effort to look nice. Be sure to wear shoes that are in good condition, and polished if leather.

- **Be well groomed and practice good hygiene.**
  If you haven't had a haircut lately, perhaps this is a good time. Of course, you will shave and shower before your date, and you'll also need to use enough deodorant to last throughout the evening. If you wear cologne, make sure that you use it sparingly and that it isn't overpowering. And don't forget to check for unsightly nose or ear hairs before you leave your home.

- **Be on time.**
  Being late for a date shows disrespect and will start the date off on a negative note. If you're going to be more than ten minutes late, call or text to let your date know. Hopefully it's for a very good reason.

- **Always open doors.**
  When a lady is about to enter your car, a restaurant, a club, or anyplace with a door, you should always hold it open for her, standing at the hinge side of the door.

- **Assist her with her coat.**
  Always offer to help a lady put on her coat. Hold it at waist level as she puts her arms in the sleeves, then pull it up after she has done so.

- **Stand up and pull out her chair.**
  If you're seated at the table when your date arrives, stand up and pull out a chair for her, then gently push it in as she sits down. When dining out, your date should be seated so she has the best view of the restaurant. If an unaccompanied lady is sitting next to you—generally on your right side at a dinner party—offer to pull out her chair as well.

- **Offer your arm.**
  When escorting a date to and from social events, you should offer her your arm. This will be greatly appreciated when walking on uneven ground, especially if she's wearing heels. The correct way to offer your arm is to bend your elbow at a right angle with your hand crossing to the front of your body. The right arm is traditionally what you offer but it matters little. Be ready to tighten your arm in case the lady slips or trips.

- **Always be courteous and complimentary.**
  Your date has made an effort to look nice for you, and your negative opinions and comments would not be welcome at this stage. Giving your date a sincere compliment about the way she looks will be greatly appreciated and let you be seen in a favorable light.

- **Choose your words carefully.**
  Show respect for your date by refraining from using coarse language or swear words.

- **At the theater or live performance.**
  If there is an usher, your date should follow the usher ahead of you. If the usher is halfway down the aisle, then you may lead the way until you reach the usher. If you have two seats at the end of an aisle, you should take the aisle seat. At the end of the performance, stand and walk up the aisle, letting your date precede you.

- **At a crowded event.**
  If moving through a crowd of people, precede your date to clear the way for her.

- **Getting into a car or taxi.**
  If it isn't safe to enter the car or taxi from the street side, you should open the door on the curb side and slide in. Your date gets in next and closes the door. If it's safe to enter on the street side, you can do so after you have opened and closed the door for the lady on the curb side of the car.

- **Be attentive at social events.**
  Do not abandon your date at social events—particularly if she doesn't know anyone at the event. Introduce her and make sure she has someone to talk to before you start mingling. And check with her occasionally to see if you can get her something to drink or eat. Show her that you care about her comfort and enjoyment.

- **Listen, make eye contact, and don't interrupt.**
  Part of showing respect is, of course, making eye contact when you're having a conversation. Your eye contact tells your date you're listening, and it actually makes you a better listener. Listening without interrupting shows interest, respect, and the ability to compromise. Make her feel as if she is the only person in the room.

- **Make small talk first.**
  If it's a first date and you don't know the person well, make small talk to break the ice and establish a connection. Be well informed. Watch the news and read newspapers so you're up to date with current affairs. Current affairs are important because they show you're interested in the world around you.

- **Avoid these subjects on a date:**
  Don't mention your health or diet habits; the cost of things; how

much money you make; mean gossip; off-color jokes; past dates or relationships; and controversial issues when you don't know the person well.

- **Turn your cell phone off.**
  Avoid taking calls and checking your messages or social media when you're with a date. You want to give the person you're with your full, undivided attention.

- **The man should pay.**
  You should pick up the dinner tab on the first date unless, of course, the woman invited you and let you know ahead of time that she would like to pay for dinner. Almost everyone I have ever asked about this topic in my social etiquette classes is in agreement that a man should pay for dinner on a first date. After that, the two can decide the course their relationship will take. It should be about more than money. Perhaps the person who has less money to pay for dinners out can cook dinner occasionally. The relationship—if there is to be one—should be reciprocal.

- **End the night on a pleasant note.**
  Even if you didn't like your date, you should treat her with respect and tell her you enjoyed spending time with her and getting to know her. And, a gentleman always makes sure his date gets safely home.

- **Follow up the next day.**
  The day after a date is often a letdown, filled with anxiety about whether there will be a second date. Will he or won't he call? Be compassionate and let her know how much you enjoyed getting to know her and that you will –or will not—be calling for another date.

- **Be discreet.**
  A gentleman never shares intimate details about his date or

any private information she may have shared with him. And, of course, you should expect the same from her.

- **Be kind.**
    If you decide a woman is not for you after seeing her for a while, have the courtesy to tell her face to face or by phone. Do not break up by text or on social media. Not only will doing so give you a bad reputation, it is extremely unkind.

32

SUCCESS

Show Consideration to Your Fellow Gym-Goers

WORKING OUT AND STAYING FIT is not only good for your health—both physically and mentally—it is also good for your career and social life. Over 93 percent of the first impression we make on others is attributed to our appearance and body language. Whether you're trying to land a job, move up in an organization, or attract a mate, you will be much more successful in doing so if you're in shape, carry yourself with poise and confidence, and are well dressed.

We are all attracted to people who look and sound fit, and we want our leaders to look as if they have the energy, enthusiasm, and commanding presence to lead us. So don't think going to the gym is a frivolous activity; it's serious business—and it's fun! And it will be more fun, as well as enjoyable, if everyone is respectful and considerate of others.

Considerate gym and fitness studio guidelines:

- **Dress in appropriate fitness attire.**
  Leave the tattered, torn, and dirty clothes at home. And cover up, please. Most people prefer not to be distracted by too much skin or too-tight workout clothes.

- **Wear deodorant but skip the cologne and aftershave.**
  In very close quarters, it's nice to work out next to someone who smells clean—not sweaty or overly fragranced.

- **Take turns, share equipment, and don't crowd.**
  If you're resting between sets on a piece of equipment and someone is waiting to use that equipment, let them work in while you rest. If the gym isn't busy and there are several of the same machine available, don't use one right next to another person.

- **Share the water fountain.**
  If someone is behind you, let them go ahead before you fill up a large water bottle. And never ever spit in the water fountain.

- **Place weights back on the rack when you finish using them.**
  It is not only thoughtful, but avoids the risk of someone tripping over them.

- **Wipe equipment with a sanitizing wipe after using it.**
  Everyone would prefer that you keep your perspiration and germs to yourself.

- **Stay home if you are sick.**
  Just as it would be inconsiderate to go to work if you're sick, it is especially inconsiderate to go to the gym, where germs can easily spread on equipment and in rooms where classes are held.

- **Show respect for others' space in classes.**
  Leave space around your mat for others to move during classes. And if you're blocking someone's view of themselves in the mirror, move your mat over.

- **Share the benches in the locker room.**
  Be considerate. Leave room for others to place their belongings on the bench while they get ready to work out or leave.

- **Take a quick shower if there are people waiting.**
  The gym is not the place for your usual ten-minute shower—particularly if there are others waiting to shower. Place your used towels in the appropriate bins when you've finished drying off.

- **Don't talk on your cell phone on the gym floor or in the locker room** — especially if there are "no cell-phone" signs. And certainly, don't take photos in the locker room.

- **Don't make loud noises.**
  Unless you're at a serious, all-male gym, refrain from grunting sounds and letting your weights slam down on the equipment or floor. Others may not appreciate hearing these sounds or other loud, distracting noises.

- **Don't interrupt classes by arriving late or leaving early.**
  If you're late to class, don't expect your favorite spot to be waiting for you; quietly take whatever spot is available. If you need to leave early, let the instructor know and stay in the back of the class so you can quietly slip out.

- **Don't bring your gym bag or personal belongings to the gym floor.**
  These items present a tripping hazard; use the lockers or coat check.

- **Don't talk loudly or carry on a long conversation in the steam room or sauna.**
  These rooms are meant for quiet relaxation, and it's hard to relax when others are talking.

- **Don't stare.**
  Whether on the gym floor or in the locker room, staring makes others feel uncomfortable, and it isn't polite.

33

SUCCESS

A Gentleman's Sport: Courteous Decorum for the Golf Course

The object of golf is not just to win. It is to play like a gentleman.
—Phil Mickelson

GOLF IS THE ULTIMATE SPORT for building personal and professional relationships. The rapport and camaraderie you build with others on the golf course can and often does lead to new business deals, as well as strengthening existing business connections. After all, what other sport or activity provides you with two to four uninterrupted hours—depending on whether you play a 9- or 18-hole round—in a peaceful setting with plenty of fresh air.

Unlike cultural events where talking is not permitted, or sporting events like football, where talking is permitted but it's too loud to hear what's being said, on a golf course you can quietly converse. If you plan to talk business while golfing, the best time to do so is on the golf cart between holes. However, never talk or move on the green or at the tee while a player is preparing to hit the ball.

10 manners to mind on the golf course:

1. **Wear the proper attire.**
   Proper golf attire is usually a collared shirt with khakis or golf slacks. Shorts are okay at some clubs, as long as they are not too short, but most golf clubs prohibit jeans. White or pastel colors are preferred over bright colors and patterns that can be distracting. Wear specific golf club shoes, which have soft spikes rather than metal spikes, along with socks that complement your clothing. Visors and baseball caps may be worn, but not straw or bucket hats.

2. **Respect the greens.**
   Avoid driving your golf cart onto soggy fairways since the cart can leave deep grooves in the grass. And be careful not to damage the putting green when putting your bag down.

3. **Repair divots and ball marks.**
   Retrieve and replace the divot by pressing it back into the divot hole and repair any ball marks you may have made. You want to leave the grounds in good shape for those following behind you.

4. **Retreive your tee.**
   Once you've hit your drive, remove your tee. If you have broken the tee, be sure to pick up all the pieces.

5. **Swing your club at the right time.**
   Always wait to swing your golf club until the group playing ahead of you is completely outside your range. If you find that your ball is heading in the direction of another player or group of players, once you've hit your ball, be sure to yell "Fore!" to signal that they should be watchful of your incoming golf ball.

6. **Never throw your golf clubs.**
   Being a gentleman means you can control your temper and that you behave in an appropriate manner. Not only is throwing your golf clubs unbefitting the gentleman's sport, it is also dangerous.

7. **Be ready when it's your turn.**
   Keep the game moving by being ready to take your shot when it's your turn. This saves time walking to and from and setting up your shot. The 'away' player (the player whose ball is farthest from the green) always hits first. When your group has finished taking their shots, move on immediately so the group behind you can continue their game. And if you're searching for a lost ball, wave ahead the next group.

8. **Know when it's time to talk and when it isn't.**
   When someone is getting ready to putt or swing their club, everyone should remain silent. You and the members of your party should also be mindful of not talking or laughing too loudly around others who may be playing closely in front or behind you. And be sure to have your cell phone turned off; or better still, leave it in the locker room.

9. **Be a good sport.**
   Praise those who may have played better than you; be gracious in accepting praise from others; and don't complain or make excuses for why you may have played better. It is also wise to refrain from analyzing or commenting on the score, the style of a partner's swing, or how they are hitting the ball.

10. **Show appreciation for your caddie.**
    Be courteous and give him the appropriate gratuity. Tips can vary depending upon the service and price of greens. If you are a guest at a club, consult with your host.

34

SUCCESS

Dignified Decorum for Attending the Opera, Ballet, Symphony or Theater

ATTENDING A LIVE PERFORMANCE SUCH as the opera, ballet, symphony, or a Broadway show is quite different from attending a sporting event. For one thing, the audience is generally more reserved and dignified—except of course at curtain call—and generally these performances are held indoors in a more intimate setting. Nearly every move you make or word you utter can impact those seated around you, and more importantly can affect the performers onstage if they become distracted by you. Show respect for the performers and audience members by following the guidelines outlined below. The same standards of decorum would apply to all live performances.

Dignified decorum for live cultural performances:

- **Dress appropriately.**
  Unless it is a gala, dress for the opera as you would the ballet: a suit and tie, or blazer with dress slacks. For a gala, the preferred attire is black tie—also known as a tuxedo, with a formal white tuxedo shirt and bow tie, black patent-leather or calfskin pumps or laced oxfords and black over the calf socks. A dark suit with a

white shirt, conservative tie, black socks, and black leather shoes would also be acceptable in some cases.

- **Be on time.**
  At most performances, you will not be seated if you arrive after the curtain has risen. You will have to wait until the intermission.

- **Check your coat, shopping bags, and briefcases.**
  The seats and rows in most theaters are very close together, leaving little or no room for any personal belongings. Be considerate of your seatmates and check anything not necessary for viewing the performance.

- **Be quiet.**
  Turn cell phones, pagers, electronic devices, watch alarms, etc. completely off. If you have a cold, use nasal spray and unwrap cough drops **before** the performance starts, or stay home. Don't talk, snore, hum, or whisper once the performance starts.

- **Don't wear too much perfume or aftershave, but be sure your breath and body smell fresh.**
  There will be individuals sitting on either side of you, and you wouldn't want to offend them.

- **Eat a small snack before you go.**
  This should avert stomach growling during the performance.

- **Don't drink too much before the performance.**
  That way you won't misbehave or need to go to the restroom.

- **Never use penlights or phone lights to read the program or libretto—the words that are sung—during the performance.**

- **Do your homework.**
  It will make the performance more enjoyable if you know the story and something about the members of the cast; and it will give you something to talk about during the intermission.

- **Sit still.**
  Do not fidget in your seat, bob your head back and forth, or tap your toes, no matter how restless you become or how tempting the pulsing rhythm of the percussion.

- **Be polite.**
  Say "please excuse me" if you need to pass in front of others to get to your seat. Face the stage as you pass, moving as quickly and delicately as you can.

- **Do not wear hats that obstruct the vision of those behind you and, no matter the discomfort, don't take off your shoes.**

- **Intermission is your opportunity to mingle and converse with others attending the performance.**
  Get up from your seat and have something to drink while you mingle. Champagne is the preferred choice of beverage at the opera.

- **Return to your seat as soon as you hear the bell ring—preferably before everyone in your row is seated.**

- **At final curtain.**
  The performers come out like heads of state, in reverse rank order—the top stars are last. This is the one time to be exuberant, but there are rules to follow, especially at the opera. When applauding women, you cheer "Brava!", accent on the last syllable. When applauding men, you cheer "Bravo!" When applauding both men and women, you cheer "Bravi."

- **Be courteous and appreciative of the performance.**
  Rather than rushing out to beat the crowds, stay to applaud the performers. For great performers, stand and applaud. This is the way we show our appreciation for their performance and all the work they did.

35

SUCCESS

Civil Conduct for Private and Commercial Air Travel

YOUR JOURNEY TO FARAWAY PLACES begins the minute you enter an airplane. Make it a pleasant one for yourself and the other passengers by behaving in the same respectful manner you would anywhere else.

Common courtesy when on an airplane:

- When you board the plane with a carry-on or shoulder bag, hold it in front of you, not at your side, as you walk down the aisle.
- When you reach your seat, quickly put one bag in the overhead bin above your seat or nearby. Be careful not to squash other people's belongings.
- If you see someone having trouble lifting a suitcase, offer to help if you can.
- If you have an aisle seat, keep your elbow and feet from protruding into the aisle.
- If the person in the aisle seat is sleeping and you need to get out of your row, softly say, "Excuse me," and if necessary, tap them lightly on the arm. It's okay to wake someone up if you do it gently.
- Keep any work materials you are using from overflowing into your seatmate's space.

- Don't read the worksheets or laptop screen of the person next to you.
- If your seatmate is reading, working, or has their eyes closed, they don't want to talk. If your seatmate would like to chat, but you wouldn't, smile and answer a few questions with a yes or no. If that doesn't work, be direct but polite: "It's been nice chatting with you. I'm going to use this time to read/work/sleep. Thanks for understanding."
- Keep noise to a minimum, whether talking with another passenger or reading to a child. If your child plays a video game or watches a movie on a laptop, use the headset or your earbuds. Your neighbor shouldn't be able to hear it.
- Don't stay longer than necessary in the lavatory, and leave the space neat and clean.
- Try not to block the view of those watching the inflight movie or other entertainment. If you must stand to retrieve something from the overhead bin, be as quick as possible.
- It's your privilege to recline your seat, but it is considerate to do so only partway or to first ask the passenger behind you if he minds.

36

SUCCESS

A Savvy Man's Guide to Hosting or Attending a Party

Host Duties:

- **Dress for the occasion.**
  Just because you are entertaining your friends and colleagues in your home, it doesn't mean you don't have to change your shirt or put on a fresh pair of slacks or shorts.

- **Let your guests know what the attire will be.**
  If you're having a formal affair and a guest arrives casually dressed, it will make feel them and your other guests feel uncomfortable.

- **Invite your neighbors.**
  If you live in an apartment building and are having a cocktail party, you might consider inviting your nearby neighbors. Otherwise, they might resent you.

- **Clean and prepare your bathrooms.**
  Put out fresh soap and hand towels, and don't forget to have extra rolls of toilet paper on hand.

- **Have ample seating.**
  Make sure you have a place for everyone to sit—even if you're entertaining outside.

- **Greet your guests.**
  Always greet guests warmly at the door with a handshake and a smile to make them feel welcome.

- **Have a place for gifts.**
  There should be a designated table for any host/hostess gifts your guests may bring.

- **Have a plan for coats.**
  Rent a coat rack with enough coat hangers for the number of guests you have invited if there isn't sufficient room in your closet for everyone's coats. You can also designate a bed to use for coats.

- **Extend your hospitality.**
  Give arriving guests directions to food and drinks. Even better, if it's a small party and you have a catering staff for the event, have a butler greet guests as they arrive with a specialty cocktail or glass of champagne.

- **Introduce guests of honor and new people.**
  Introduce guests to any guests they may not know. If there's a guest of honor, you can either walk around the party introducing him or her to other guests, or you can make a formal announcement to everyone at the same time.

- **Encourage conversation among your guests.**
  After all guests arrive, you should circulate to make sure everyone has someone to talk to and is enjoying themselves.

- **Replenish and tidy the food and beverage areas.**
  Assign someone to periodically make sure you have enough food and drinks out for the duration of the party, and to check that the serving areas and food platters still look tidy and no soiled cocktail napkins are lying around.

- **If necessary, make arrangements for guests to get home safely.**
  If a guest has had too much to drink and is planning to drive home, it is your responsibility as the host to see that they have another means of getting there.

- **Stand by the door at the end of the party.**
  Always say goodbye to your guests and shake hands with them before they leave.

- **R.S.V.P.**
  Do respond to an invitation you receive from your host, even if it's a Facebook invitation. Regrets are just as important for the host to know about as acceptances. And once you have said you will attend, it would be very rude not to show up.

Guest Manners

- **Never bring any uninvited guests, including friends, your children, or your dog, to an affair without asking the host's permission first.**

- **Do not expect the host to cater to your specific dietary needs.**
  If you have food allergies, it's a good idea to let your host know when he extends the invitation to you. Most hosts now ask their guests in advance if they have any special dietary concerns.

- **Dress appropriately.**
  If you're unsure of what to wear for the occasion, call your host and ask. Wearing the appropriate attire is a mark of respect to the party host.

- **Host/hostess gift.**
  Always take a gift for the host or hostess if you're going to their home for dinner or a special cocktail party. Fresh flowers are not a good idea, but a plant would be nice, as would a box of candy, candles, cocktail napkins, etc.

- **Greet your host first.**
  Always say hello to the host as soon as you arrive—before enjoying their hospitality (drinks and food).

- **Introduce yourself.**
  Don't hesitate to introduce yourself to the other guests, and shake hands when you meet them.

- **Introduce others.**
  If you're having a conversation and someone you don't know walks up, introduce yourself, then introduce the person with whom you were talking.

- **Be sociable.**
  Circulate, mingle, and converse with the other guests at the party. Make an effort to shine and you will be invited back. Spend the evening on your cell phone and, more than likely, you won't be invited back.

- **If you spill or break something, let the host know immediately.**
  Offer to help clean it up. It's your responsibility to pay for something you have broken.

- **Thank the host before you leave.**
  If you have to leave early, however, let your host know that when you arrive and that you will call them the next day to express your thanks.

- **Follow up.**
  The day after the party, call or send the host a handwritten thank-you note.

37

SUCCESS

Houseguest Guidelines for Enjoyable Visits with Family and Friends

Host Duties

- Do invite guests whom you know fairly well and are sure will enjoy the kind of weekend that is enjoyable to you.
- Tell your guests when you would like for them to arrive and leave.
- Give your guests an idea of what you have planned for the weekend and the clothes they will need to bring for the various activities. If you are taking them to your club for dinner and jackets are required, that is something they will need to know when packing for the weekend.
- If you're inviting friends to your home whom you don't know well, it's a good idea to ask if they have any special dietary needs or allergies.
- Do stock your kitchen and bar with your guests' favorite foods and drinks.
- Give your guests some free time during the day. It isn't necessary—nor is necessarily appreciated by your guests—for you to have every minute of the day planned. Do, however, have some group outings/activities planned.

- Let your guests know what time you usually have your meals—particularly breakfast. If you're a late sleeper and they are early risers, show them where you keep the coffee and let them know they are welcome to make their own breakfast.
- Give your guests a map of your town if they are new to the area.
- Check to make sure the guest room is ready before your guests arrive: fresh sheets, flowers, snacks, reading material, an alarm clock, pad and pen by the bed, a couple of empty bureau drawers, extra clothes hangers in the closet, a mirror, and anything else you think might help them be comfortable. Also, make sure the bathroom they will use has everything they'll need in it.
- Do let your guests know if there is a limited supply of hot water in your house. They will be embarrassed if they unknowingly use up all the hot water before others in the house have had a chance to shower.
- Try to anticipate your guests' special needs—if there are any. As a host, it is your number one responsibility to make your guests feel comfortable in your home.

Houseguest Manners

- Do be clear about when you are expected to arrive and leave, and don't go earlier or stay longer.
- Do take a house gift and, if you're staying longer than a weekend, offer to take your host out to dinner one evening.
- If possible, have a means of transportation so you don't have to rely on your host to chauffeur you around.
- Do not ask to bring a pet with you unless you have a small, perfectly-behaved dog and you know your host won't mind. Large dogs and cats should be left at home.
- If you or your children are sick, let your host know before heading out to their house. Of course, It would be better if you visited another time, but your host–and certainly a relative–may say it's okay for you to come.

- Ask what the attire will be for the weekend so that you're able to dress appropriately for all of the weekend's festivities and will not have to borrow clothes from your host.
- Unless your host has a full staff, you should put your breakfast dishes in the dishwasher and offer to strip the bed when it's time for you to leave.
- Do think of activities to occupy you for at least part of the day. Don't expect your host to keep you entertained from morning till night—unless you know your host is expecting you to accompany them on all of their outings during the day, such as to the golf course, tennis court, beach, ski slope, etc.
- Do not leave your wet bath or sandy beach towels on the floor.
- Do try to keep your room fairly neat. Make your own bed each morning unless there's a maid to make it for you. Be sure to keep the bathroom neat as well.
- Do pack a robe. You may have to walk down the hall to go to the bathroom; and you may want to wear one to breakfast if it's acceptable in the house you're visiting.
- Ask what the rules of the house are. Are shoes allowed inside? What time does everyone wake up and go to sleep?
- Do not treat your hosts as your personal servants. Offer to help out with the cooking and dishes.
- If you are a weekend guest, do realize that it is not your host's responsibility to keep you entertained every minute of the day.
- Don't expect your hosts to follow your diet regimen. If you are on a strict diet, it might be better to save your visit to another time when you can eat what your hosts are eating.
- Be on time for meals and activities.
- Don't complain about your bed, your room, the food, the activities that have been planned for your stay, etc. In other words, be an appreciative guest.
- On the day of your departure, take the sheets, blankets, and pillow cases off the bed, fold them, and leave them neatly on top

of the bed—unless, of course, your hosts have live-in help or tell you they would prefer that you leave everything to them.

- Do remember to send a thank-you note to your host when you get home.

38

> SUCCESS

Make a Favorable Impression at the Table

The real test of table manners is never to offend the sensibilities of others.
—Emily Post

WHEN IT COMES TO DINING, there is no better or possibly worse place to make an impression than at the table. It is absolutely essential that, if you want to be at your personal best at the table, you will need to have polished dining skills and impeccable table manners. Of course, finessing the art of the meal—fine dining skills, good table manners, etc.—may take practice, but once you've mastered this art, you will have the grace and refinement to dine with anyone, anywhere in the world.

Good table manners are about showing a sensitive awareness of others at the table, and conducting oneself in a way that makes the dining experience a pleasant one for everyone involved. Some of the rules for the table were devised for the safety of the diner, and others to make the act of eating more attractive. The best table manners are unaffected, making those around you feel comfortable.

It is food that brings together friends and families after a long day at work or school. It is food that brings us together to celebrate all the special occasions in our lives—weddings, graduations, christenings, birthdays, bar mitzvahs, holidays, and promotions. And today, nearly half of all business transactions, including job interviews, are conducted at the table. If you are unfamiliar with formal table settings and how to properly eat the various courses, you may find the experience of dining with others stressful and unenjoyable.

Children who have good table manners are always welcome at the table—whether at home, at school, or in a restaurant. If you are a parent, I recommend instilling the importance of having good table manners in your children as soon as they are able to join you at the table. They should be encouraged to practice their table manners just as they are encouraged to practice sports or musical instruments. And whenever possible, parents should join their children for meals and conversation.

For a comprehensive guide to dining, I recommend my book, *The Art of Dining Well—Everything You Need to Know to Shine at the Table*.

Patricia's Top 20 Rules for the Table

1. Wait until everyone has been served to begin eating—unless your host tells you to start or you are with a large party.
2. Avoid talking with food in your mouth.
3. Chew your food quietly with your mouth closed.
4. Wait until you have swallowed the food in your mouth and dabbed your mouth with your napkin before taking a sip of your beverage.
5. Cut and eat one piece of meat at a time.
6. Never lick your fingers. Wipe your fingers and mouth with your napkin.
7. Once you have taken your silverware off the table and used it, it should never touch the table again. Place it on your plate in either the resting or finished position.
8. Bring your food to your mouth when you eat; do not bend your head down to your food.
9. Don't reach over someone's plate for something; ask for the item to be passed.
10. Never spear food off another person's plate with your fork.

11. Pass food and other items to the right, or counterclockwise, at the table.
12. Always pass the salt and pepper together. They are "married" and never separated.
13. Use a utensil instead of your fingers unless you are eating finger foods. Never use your fingers to push food onto your spoon or fork; use your knife.
14. Avoid spreading your elbows when cutting. Keep them close to your sides.
15. Eat at a similar pace as the others at the table. Do not eat too quickly or too slowly.
16. Never pick food out of your teeth at the table.
17. If you need to blow your nose, excuse yourself and go to the restroom; and certainly, do not use your napkin.
18. Do not place your cell phone, keys, glasses, or handbag on the table.
19. Do not answer your cell phone or text on it while you are at the table.
20. Always thank the host at the end of the meal.

39

How to Host a Flawless Meal at a Restaurant

The top 10 entertaining tips:

1. **Start by selecting a restaurant with which you are familiar.**
   It should offer superior service, excellent food, and be convenient for your guest or guests. Knowing the restaurant and staff will make you feel more confident about hosting the meal.

2. **Arrive early and choose a table.**
   Seating and table location are very important considerations, especially for business meals. Request a table away from the kitchen, restrooms, bar, entryway or middle of the restaurant.

3. **Prior to taking a seat, decide the chair location for your guest or guests.**
   If there is more than one guest, the most important guest should be seated to the right of the host; the second most important guest is on the host's left, unless there is a co-host. If so, the second most important guest would be seated to the co-host's right. If you are hosting a lady for a social meal, be sure to give her the seat with the best view of the restaurant.

4. **Stand when guests arrive, shake hands, and let them know where you would like them to sit.**

5. **As host, you may want to make suggestions from the menu.**
   Suggestions ease the guest's uncertainty about what to order, lets them know what dishes are best at the restaurant, and gives them an idea of the number of courses you are considering. To make your guest or guests feel comfortable, you should order the same number of courses they order.

6. **At a business lunch, opt for easy-to-eat dishes that require a knife and fork to eat.**
   Anything that is messy should be avoided. Practice good table manners while dining, remembering to swallow before speaking and chewing with your lips closed. Pace yourself so that you and your guest are finished at the same time.

7. **Manage drinks orders.**
   Let your guest know it's okay for them to drink whatever they like by asking, "Would you like to order a beverage?' It's okay to have an alcoholic drink if your guest abstains, but no more than one is recommended at a business lunch.

8. **Avoid getting down to business as soon as you are seated.**
   Conversation during the early part of the meal should be about building rapport with your guest. Save serious business for later in the meal, after the entrée plates have been removed. If you're hosting a more social meal, conversation should be about topics like current events—if not controversial—vacations, hobbies, sports, etc.

9. **The host pays the bill, which includes the gratuity, which is generally 20 percent of the bill before tax if at a fine dining restaurant.**
   As the host, you are also responsible for your guest's coat check and valet parking tips as well.

10. **Signal the end of the meal by placing your napkin on the table and rising from your chair.**
    If it's a social meal and there are ladies present, you should pull out the chairs for them. This doesn't apply to a business meal, where men are not expected to help female executives.

Ordering Wine at a Restaurant

When selecting a wine from a restaurant's wine list, the main goal is to accomplish a suitable pairing with the entrees of your party. If the food orders are too different to be compatible with one wine, consider purchasing splits or ordering by the glass. Waiters and sommeliers are there to answer your questions, so don't hesitate to ask for their advice. No one knows the wine list or the food menu as well as the people who work in the restaurant, and their insights can steer you to the best wine and food pairing.

- **The sommelier's job.**
  A sommelier is the person whose job it is to create the wine list and help people find their way through it. And it's their job to ensure that all of the items on the menu have wines that can be paired with them.

- **Your job as host.**
  A sommelier is there to assist you. All you need to do is ask for his help and provide him with the following information: What you are having to eat; how much you want to spend; what you have in mind, if anything; and what sort of wine you typically enjoy—red, white, a little sweet, bone-dry, etc.

- **Have a Taste.**
  The wine person or waiter will pour a little wine into your glass and then stand there waiting for your approval. After you, the host, have taken a sip and given your approval, the waiter will move onto the next person and fill everyone's glasses, coming

back to you last. He will fill the glasses only half full, depending upon the size of the glass, to allow you room to swirl the wine without getting it on you or the tablecloth. Guests should wait to take a drink until you have lifted your glass.

- **Holding a Wine Glass.**
 A champagne or white wine glass should be held by the stem, and a red wine glass by the bowl. When you hold a glass by the bowl, your hand warms the wine, which is okay for a red wine, but not a white wine or champagne that has been properly chilled.

- **Refusing to Have Wine.**
 If wine is being served and you do not care for any, place your fingertips lightly on the rim of the glass when the server approaches to pour. Or you can simply say, "No, thank you." Do not turn your glass upside down.

The Perfect Toast for Special Occasions

The perfect toast is short, funny, and heartfelt. Three minutes is the ideal length for a toast, and it generally follows a basic structure:

- **Stand.**
 Begin by standing up if you are at a large gathering or sitting at a table with a dozen or more guests. Do not clink your glass to get their attention; simply raise your glass toward the center of the room to indicate you're about to begin.

- **The hook.**
 Start with something compelling about the person being toasted.

- **Background.**
 Give a brief background of yourself to let guests know why you are giving the toast and how you're connected to the person you're toasting.

- **Tell a story.**
  Tell one or two stories or anecdotes about the person you're toasting, Funny is good, but avoid stories that would embarrass the person or make the guests uncomfortable. The stories or anecdotes should be appropriate for the audience.

- **The end.**
  Ask the audience or guests attending the event to raise their glasses with you to the person being toasted. You can ask them to stand if you choose to do so.

GRATUITY GUIDE IN THE U.S.A.

Maitre d'	$5.00 – $20.00
Captain	5% of the dinner tab
Restaurant Server	15 – 20% of the dinner
Sommelier (Wine Steward)	$3.00 – $5.00 or 20% of tab
Bartender	15 – 20% of bar tab
Restaurant Attendant	$1.00
Coat Clerk	$1.00 – $2.00 per coat
Parking Valet	$1.00 – $3.00
Doorman (when he hails a taxi for you)	$1.00 – $2.00
Taxi Cab Driver	15 to 20% of the bill

40

| SUCCESS |

Show Your Appreciation with a Thoughtful Thank-You Note

Feeling gratitude and not expressing it is like wrapping a present and not sending it.

—William Arthur Ward

ALWAYS BE APPRECIATIVE AND EXPRESS your gratitude with a thank-you note when someone does something for you, gives you a gift, or has you as a guest in their home. Of course, not every kind gesture will require a written thank-you note; but it will always require an acknowledgement of the gesture. Simply saying thank-you often suffices; but depending upon the magnitude of the gesture or favor, you may want to do something reciprocal for the person.

Ideally, a thank-you note should be sent within 48 hours. It shows your sincerity when you send it promptly. However, a note sent later is better than not sending one at all. And, although a hand-written note will always be valued above an electronic note, any note will be much appreciated today. Consider the person you are sending your note to—a grandmother, or a twenty-something. In which format would they most enjoy receiving your note?

- **Wedding gift thank-you notes.**
  According to wedding gift etiquette, you have up to three months to send thank-you notes, although notes sent upon receipt of gifts often seem and sound more sincere. You and your partner should participate in writing the notes—particularly if you received many gifts and both of you have busy schedules. If you received a material gift, mention the item in your note. For example, "We plan to use your vase on our new entry-way table." If you have received a cash gift, let the giver know how you plan to use it, such as "Your generous gift will go toward the purchase of furniture for our new house."

- **Write your note on good-quality stationery with matching envelopes.**
  Foldover note cards are more often used for personal thank-you notes—especially for wedding gifts—but you can also use correspondence cards. Do not use fill-in-the-blanks cards for any notes. They are meant more for children and show a lack of discernment on your part. You will also need to have a good quality fountain or ballpoint pen, the latter being a little less elegant. Use only black or blue ink for your notes.

- **The note format and the envelope.**
  Thank-you notes need not be long, Three or four carefully crafted, warm and heartfelt sentences will be perfect. Your note will include a salutation: Dear Aunt Lucinda; your three-or-four sentence message; and a signature, such as Love, Bill and Agnes. The envelope should be addressed with the title and full name of the person: Mr. and Mrs. Ed Jones and their address. Your return address goes on the back flap of the envelope since it is a personal note.

41

SUCCESS

Pursue Culture to Enrich Yourself and Become a More Interesting, Knowledgeable Man

IN ADDITION TO NOURISHING YOUR inner self, reading noteworthy books, touring art museums, and attending live cultural events will make you a more interesting, knowledgeable person. By being well versed in culture, history, and the world around you, you will have something to talk about with whomever you encounter socially or professionally. Besides, it's fun to learn new things and acquire knowledge for its own sake and to broaden your horizons. Although not necessarily a prerequisite for a successful life, worldliness is an attractive asset to possess. It will give you a certain savoir-faire appeal.

Best not to be pretentious about the knowledge you acquire however; nor should you be a show-off to impress someone. Your study and appreciation of the finer things in life is for your own improvement and to share with other like-minded people when the situation arises. As Warren Buffet has often said, "By far the best investment you can make is in yourself." That means never stop acquiring knowledge that betters you as a whole person. Buffet believes his lifelong pursuit of knowledge is the secret sauce of his success.

By far the best investment you can make is in yourself.

I highly recommend The Great Courses for learning about culture. I have taken several courses, including mythology, opera, and Shakespeare. You can fit them into your schedule by listening to the audio versions when working out, commuting to work, or traveling.

Following is a "Good-to-Know" list. Don't be intimidated by it. It is, in fact, not even a complete list of everything it would be good to know, study, or do to be a cultured man; It is simply a sampling of areas or topics you might want to become familiar with or pursue in greater depth when you have the time or interest. Keep in mind, knowledge is a lifelong pursuit: carve out time to educate your eye and ear, realizing that you will have more time for these pursuits when you get older and more established in your career.

The Good-to-Know List: An Introduction

I. Literature
Reading is both relaxing and stimulating at the same time. To be a great leader, you must always be willing to broaden your world and increase your knowledge. The learning you gain from reading greatly increases your self-satisfaction and potential to succeed.

- **The Classics**

    10 of the greatest novels of all time:
    Anna Karenina by Leo Tolstoy, *Madame Bovary* by Gustave Flaubert, *War and Peace* by Leo Tolstoy, *The Great Gatsby* by F. Scott Fitzgerald, *Middlemarch* by George Eliot, *Stories of Anton Chekhov* by Anton Chekov; *In Search of Lost Time* by Marcel Proust, *Moby Dick* by Herman Melville, *Death in Venice* by Thomas Mann, *Heart of Darkness* by Joseph Conrad

- **Playwrights**

  Shakespeare
  William Shakespeare is considered the world's greatest playwright. He wrote 37 plays in the 16th century, many of which are still performed today because they are timeless with a universality that everyone can relate to. He is so frequently quoted and referenced that it would be a very good idea to become familiar with his most famous plays.

  Shakespeare's plays fall into four categories: histories, comedies, tragedies, and romances. His 10 most famous plays are: *Hamlet, Macbeth, Romeo and Juliet, A Midsummer Night's Dream, King Lear, The Tempest, Much Ado About Nothing, Othello, Twelfth Night,* and *The Merchant of Venice.*

  Best playwrights of all time:
  William Shakespeare, Arthur Miller, Tennessee Williams, Eugene O'Neill, Henrik Ibsen, Anton Chekhov, Samuel Beckett, Oscar Wilde, George Bernard Shaw, Sam Shepard, Sophocles, Tom Stoppard, Neil Simon, Noel Coward, David Mamet, David Hare, Tony Kushner, August Wilson, Bertolt Brecht, Edward Albee

- **Greek Mythology**

  The major Greek gods and goddesses to know:
  Zeus, god of the sky and thunder. As the chief Greek deity, Zeus is considered the ruler, protector, and father of all gods and humans; Hera, goddess or women, marriage, family, and childbirth; Hephaestus, god of fire; Aphrodite, goddess of love; Ares, god of war; Athena, goddess of wisdom; Poseidon, god of the sea, earthquakes, and horses; Artemis, goddess of the hunt and all newborn creatures; Apollo, god of music, light and reason;

Hermes, god of shepherds, travelers, merchants, thieves, and all others who live by their wits; Hades, lord of the dead; Demeter, goddess of the harvest; Persephone, goddess of the underworld and of spring growth; Dionysus, god of wine.

Note: You may also want to know the Roman names for the gods.

- **Current Literature**
Many news publications such as *The New York Times, The Boston Globe, The Seattle Times, The Christian Science Monitor* to name a few, h*ave* a book review section which is a source for current noteworthy and bound-to-be-talked about books. At a minimum, you should strive to read one book a month, although one book a week would be ideal. If you spend a lot of time commuting to work, the good news is that most books now have an audio version, so you can listen to a book while driving.

- **Newspapers**
This is a must: to read at least one newspaper every day, either online or in print. If you don't know what's going on locally, nationally, and around the world, you'll seem self-interested and egocentric rather than well-informed and sophisticated.

- **Magazines**
Magazines, such as *Newsweek, The New Yorker, Time, and People magazine,* are wonderful sources for human interest stories. You can read current, in-depth articles about your field in targeted industry publications. As with newspapers, most, if not all magazines are online now, so you can view and read them more easily. Apple News has a subscription plan that includes a wide array of magazines at a very affordable cost.

II. The Performing Arts

- **Opera**

    10 of the most notable operas and their composers are:
    Carmen by Georges Bizet, *Madame Butterfly* by Giacomo Puccini, *La Traviata* by Giuseppe Verdi, *La Bohème* by Giacomo Puccini, *The Marriage of Figaro* by Wolfgang Amadeus Mozart, *Don Giovanni* by Wolfgang Amadeus Mozart, *Tosca* by Giacomo Puccini, Aida by Giuseppe Verdi, *The Barber of Seville* by Gioachino Rossini, *Rigoletto* by Giuseppe Verdi.

- **Opera Singers**

    Notable contemporary classical opera singers:
    Luciano Pavarotti, Enrico Caruso, José Carreras, Maria Callas, Joan Sutherland, Placido Domingo, Renee Fleming, Dmitri Hvorostovsky, Kathleen Battle, Kiri te Kanawa, Jessye Norman

    Notable contemporary pop opera singers:
    Andrea Bocelli, Sarah Brightman, Josh Groban, Katherine Jenkins, Emma Shapplin, Susan Boyle, Nana Mouskouri, Il Divo, Celtic Woman, Luciano Pavarotti, José Carreras

Music

- **Classical music**

    Notable composers of the 18th century:
    Ludwig van Beethoven, Johann Sebastian Bach, George Frideric Handel, Wolfgang Amadeus Mozart, Pyotr Ilyich Tchaikovsky

    Notable composers of the 19th century:
    Frédéric Chopin, Franz Liszt, Franz Schubert, Richard Wagner,

Johannes Brahms. Gustav Mahler, Hector Berlioz, Sergei Rachmaninoff, Antonín Dvořák

Notable composers of the 20th century:
Claude Debussy, Maurice Ravel, Richard Strauss, Igor Stravinsky, Leonard Bernstein, George Gershwin, John Williams, Dmitri Shostakovich, Sergei Prokofiev

- **Broadway Shows**

Most famous Broadway plays:
Hamilton, The Producers, The Phantom of the Opera, The Book of Mormon, Wicked, Les Miserables, West Side Story, Kinky Boots, Fiddler on the Roof, Chicago, Cats, Hello Dolly, Miss Saigon, Mamma Mia, The Lion King, Oklahoma

- **Ballet**

Notable ballet dancers of the 20th Century:
Vaslav Nijinsky, Anna Pavlova, Margot Fonteyn, Rudolf Nureyev, Mikhail Baryshnikov, Natalia Makarova, Edward Villella, Anthony Dowell, Gelsey Kirkland, Sylvia Guillem, Alessandra Ferri, Nina Ananiashvili

Notable ballet dancers of the 21st Century:
Olga Smirnova, Alina Cojocaru, Tamara Rojo, Sergei Polunin, Marcello Gomes, Wendy Whelan, Ángel Corella, Gillian Murphy.

- **Modern Dance**

Notable modern dancers of the Twentieth Century:
Lester Horton, Katherine Dunham, Jack Cole, Gene Kelly, Jerome Robbins, Matt Mattox, Isadora Duncan, Bob Fosse, Frank

Hatchett, David Winters. Mia Michaels, Paul Taylor, Alvin Ailey, Merce Cunningham, Martha Graham

III. The Visual Arts

- **Painters: From the Renaissance to Pop Art**

    Notable painters through the ages:
    Leonarda da Vinci, Vincent van Gogh, Rembrandt, Claude Monet, Auguste Renoir, Pablo Picasso, Michelangelo, Raphael, Jan Vermeer, Salvador Dali, Andy Warhol, Jackson Pollock, Rene Magritte, Henri Matisse. Eduard Manet, Georges Seurat, Caravaggio, Goya, Edvard Munch, Edward Hopper, Frida Kahlo, Roy Lichtenstein, Gustav Klimt, Edgar Degas, Paul Cézanne

- **Sculptors**

    Notable sculptors of all time:
    Michelangelo, Gian Lorenzo Bernini, Auguste Rodin, Henry Moore,
    Constantin Brancusi, Alberto Giacometti, Sol LeWitt, Donatello, Louise Bourgeois, Alexander Calder, Fernando Botero, Barbara Hepworth, Richard Serra, Niki de Saint Phalle, Louise Nevelson

- **Photographers**

    Notable photographers of all time:
    Ansel Adams, Robert Capa, Henri Cartier Bresson, Man Ray, Robert Frank, Walker Evans, Edouard Henri Lartique, Robert Doisneau, Dorothea Lange, Diane Arbus, Alfred Stieglitz, Edward Steichen, Alfred Eisenstaedt, Margaret Bourke-White, Richard Avedon, Irving Penn

- **Architects**

    Some of the most notable architects from the 16th to 20th century:
    Michelangelo, Sir Christopher Wren, Le Corbusier, Antoni Gaudí, Ludwig Mies van der Rohe, Frank Lloyd Wright, I.M. Pei, Philip Johnson, Buckminster Fuller, Norman Foster

    Some of the most notable 21st century architects:
    Frank Gehry, I.M. Pei, Zaha Hadid, Renzo Piano, Jean Nouvel, Sir David Chipperfield, Santiago Calatrava, Moshe Safdie, Peter Zumthor, Tom Wright, Daniel Libeskind

    World famous museums to know and visit:
    The Louvre in Paris, Uffizi Gallery in Florence, The Prado in Madrid, Metropolitan Museum of Art in New York, The National Gallery in London, The National Gallery of Art in Washington, D.C., Vatican Museums in Vatican City, Tate Modern in London, State Hermitage in St. Petersburg, Museum of Modern Art in New York, Victoria and Albert Museum in London, Pompidou Centre in Paris, Guggenheim Museum in Bilbao and New York

IV. Current Affairs: Local, National, and the World

Be a citizen of the world. Spend time each day learning about what is going on around you. You never want to appear clueless. Form a habit of scheduling this 'activity' around the same time each day.

V. Sports and Sports Figures

Keep current on whatever sport is in season. Know which teams are in the championships. Know who the top players are. Even if you don't like some or any sports, this information will make you look tuned in and able to participate in a sports-related conversation.

VI. History: Local, National and World

Studying history will give you a frame of reference for current events. It will also help you understand how the past has shaped global, national, and local relationships between societies/cultures today. In addition, occasionally review world geography; geography puts history in context, and geographical regions can change rapidly as countries are renamed and/or reshaped by war.

VII. La Dolce Vita

Enjoy the sweet life and all that it has to offer in the form of food, beverages, and fine dining. Broaden your horizons and familiarize yourself with the cuisine of other cultures.

- **Beverages:** Wine, champagne, cocktails, microbrewery beers, and sparkling mineral waters.
- **Food from different cultures:** French, Italian, Greek, Japanese, Chinese, Indian, Thai, and so on.
- **Caviar and other fancy foods, such as oysters, escargot, and pâté de fois gras.**
- **Restaurants.** Fine dining in restaurants will become part of your life if you are in a client-facing business. It's a good practice to keep up with the Michelin star and trendy restaurants for when you need to entertain an important client, V.I.P, or special person.

VIII. Travel

Wherever you go, the experience adds to your savoir faire and global citizen persona. Plus, it helps you "sharpen the saw." Be sure to visit the art galleries, museums, and libraries in your area and in other cities and countries where you spend time.

IX. Your field of study or work.

Never stop studying and keeping current with advancements and news in your chosen field.

Made in United States
Troutdale, OR
12/31/2023